Charles Brague, Jean-Leon Gerome

Drawing Course

Charles Brague, Jean-Leon Gerome

Drawing Course

ISBN/EAN: 9783744651479

Printed in Europe, USA, Canada, Australia, Japan

Cover: Foto ©Thomas Meinert / pixelio.de

More available books at **www.hansebooks.com**

Charles Bargue

with the collaboration of

Jean-Léon
Gérôme

DRAWING
COURSE

Drawing 7.
Study for *The Opinion of
the Model*. (*Étude pour
L'Avis du modèle*.)
The Walters Art Museum,
Baltimore, Maryland
24.8 x 16.5 cm.
(9.75 x 6.5 in.)

CONTENTS

PREFACE AND ACKNOWLEDGMENTS

This book is dedicated to Daniel Graves for several good reasons, the most important being that he was the instigator, facilitator, and mentor for the book. From the beginnings of our friendship—some thirty years old—we talked about republishing the Bargue-Gérôme *Drawing Course*. The only complete set known to us at the time was in the National Art Library, Victoria and Albert Museum, London. Eventually both Mark Walker, the late and lamented scholar of Bouguereau, and Daniel separately photographed the plates of the *Drawing Course*, and prints from their negatives were soon circulating among a small group of artists. I enumerated to Daniel the difficulties in doing a new edition: the course had no text, and although it was self-evident that these were beautiful drawings—inspiring and exemplary models that any figurative artist would prize and want to copy—I as an art historian and not a trained artist found it hard to imagine my writing an explanation of the plates and their use.

After Daniel and Charles Cecil had opened their atelier in Florence, Daniel was able to make me the following offer: "Come to Florence and study in our atelier. I can't make an artist out of you, but I can teach you how to draw, and I can help you write the commentary for the plates." My first semester at the school was in 1983. Right off the bat I was given a plumb line, an easel, a cast of a foot in a shadow box, and was shown the rudiments of the sight-size technique. I was soon confronted by a model, whom I approached with my plumb line and chalk and the bit of experience I had gained in drawing the foot. Both Daniel and Charles—to whom I owe infinite thanks—treated me seriously as a "prospective artist." Both of them enjoyed the fact that I had had no previous training and consequently had little to unlearn. Each day they looked at my work, discussed it with me, criticized it, encouraged me, and pushed me along to the next step. It was a type of personal instruction I had never experienced and, sad to say, had never practiced in my teaching career. I was in a room with a dozen other students, and they, too, helped me with technical matters of the most elementary sort—for instance, how to sharpen my chalk, or how to place my easel. The moments of silence and discussion among the students were equally inspiring. By all accounts a hardened art historian and theoretician, I was suddenly being initiated into how artists worked, thought, and saw. Following my initiation period, Daniel and Charles spent several evenings going over the plates of the *Drawing Course* with me. I made notations on one of the first portable computers. The notes I took then became the foundation of the commentaries in this book. So, Dan, here is your book. Charles, I hope you find it useful, too. You may both find it difficult to recognize your own words through the multitudinous revisions of the text, but it is their spirit and your teachings about how to look at the drawings that animate most of the text.

The writing of several books already under way prevented my immediate return to Florence and my resumption of the study of drawing. Nonetheless, I continued to draw in studio classes in the schools where I taught in the United States, and I also drew —most informally—with several groups of professional artists in Los Angeles, who patiently accepted my amateur standing while I learned more about their working habits. My gratitude here to sculptors John Frame and Judy Debrowsky, whose studios served as the sites for these weekly meetings.

In 1996 I went back to Florence, and for five years thereafter I spent a winter or spring semester at the Florence Academy. I gave several lectures—usually on great academic masters—and continued as a student, drawing *académies* in the mornings and working from casts or copying Bargue drawings in the afternoon. At the academy I was aided by many splendid artists who daily, in turn, criticized my work—Charles Weed, Maureen Hyde, Simona Dolci, Kevin Gorges, Angelo Ramirez Sanchez, Andrea Smith, among others—all of whom were patient, aware of my intentions and abilities, as well as my limitations. The ideas, methods, and sometimes even the very words of these teachers have worked their way into this book. I borrowed shamelessly:

from Kevin Gorges's discussions about what one learned from copying master drawings; from Charles Weed's critiques about the underlying reasons for using certain techniques; from the precise and thoughtful instructions of Simona Dolci and Maureen Hyde about the necessity of self-criticism and "getting it right." Among my student companions, a special acknowledgment must be given to Polly Liu, who always knew how to help out in a pinch.

These ideas, comments, and suggestions were all augmented and revised by me to give the text a consistency of voice and method. Here I was helped by my assistant, Graydon Parrish, an artist of great learning and intelligence, who regularly gave up months of his valuable studio time to sit beside me and go over every paragraph of the book. He contributed whole passages to the technical sections as well as drawing illustrations for the appendix; he constantly checked or questioned my vocabulary and helped to consolidate my various notes for the plates. We worked very closely, and he criticized and helped with all parts of the book. We often disagreed but, needless to say, our friendship has survived intact.

Many artists among my friends were interested in the project; a small number—Jon Swihart, Kevin Gorges, Peter Bougie, Tom Knechtel, and Wes Christensen—read the manuscript in its penultimate stage and offered intelligent criticism. Many other artists, eager to see the Drawing Course published and to give it to their students, have encouraged me through the years. I thank them all. My friends in Minneapolis—especially Annette Lesueur and Peter Bougie—sustained and encouraged me during the long travail.

I was also aided by my academic colleagues, dealers, and collectors. My colleague Frances Pohl carefully read through the final draft. The most wonderful example of how art historians work together is exemplified in the section of this book on Bargue's death: documents of great importance were discovered and forwarded to me by Madeleine Beaufort and Judith Schubb in Paris and by Eric Zafran and DeCourcy E. McIntosh in the United States. In Cincinnati John Wilson did detective work into the history of the Cincinnati Art Museum. The London and New York staffs of the auction houses Christie's and Sotheby's were generous with their time and always responsive in locating information and illustrations for the book. The administration and staff of the Goupil Museum in Bordeaux—in particular Hélène Lafont-Couturier and Pierrre-Lin Renié—were of crucial importance in terms of the physical production of the book. They supplied illustrations and information I requested at a pestiferous rate and arranged for the photographing of the plates of the Drawing Course from the two complete sets owned by the museum. Sylvie Aubenas and her staff at the Bibliothèque nationale in Paris found photographs of lost paintings by Bargue in obscure locations within the library. The staffs at the Huntington Library in San Marino and the Getty Research Center in Los Angeles, California, were especially helpful; in particular, I want to thank Linda Zechler at the first institution and Mark Henderson at the second. To the countless other librarians, registrars, curators, and collectors who in one way or another added to the information, richness, and accuracy of this book I extend my thanks and gratitude for your cheerful assistance. Curators at museums in England and the United States have done valiant work for me. The staff of the Dahesh Museum of Art—associate director Michael Fahlund, curator Stephen Edidin, associate curator Roger Diederen, and curatorial research assistant Frank Verpoorten—has provided unflagging assistance and advice both as colleagues and good friends. Last but not least, Monsieur and Madame Ahmed Rafif, my publishers, have given me the wonderful support and leeway that I have enjoyed for twenty years. It was Monsieur Rafif's genial and generous idea to add the catalogue of Bargue's paintings to this edition of the Drawing Course. Above all, thanks to my partner, Leonard Simon, for his patience throughout the writing and production of another book.

THE HISTORY OF THE *DRAWING COURSE*

NTRODUCTION

The Bargue-Gérôme *Drawing Course (Cours de dessin)*, reproduced here in its entirety, is a famous and fabled publication of the late nineteenth century. Divided into three parts, it contains 197 loose-leaf lithographic plates of precise drawings after casts, master drawings, and male models, all arranged in a somewhat progressive degree of difficulty.[1] The course was designed to prepare beginning art students copying these plates to draw from nature, that is, from objects, both natural and man-made, in the real world. Like the curriculum of the nineteenth-century École des Beaux-Arts in Paris, whose ideals it shared, it was designed so that the student using it could eventually choose to render nature in both idealistic and realistic fashions. When the *Drawing Course* was published in the late 1860s, it was still generally assumed that the imitation of nature was the principal goal of the artist, and that the most important subject for the artist was the human body. The expression of the subject depicted had not yet been replaced by self-expression.

Despite being both rare and arcane today, the Bargue-Gérôme *Drawing Course* is one of the most significant documents of the last great flowering of figure painting in western art, which took place in the late nineteenth century. The present complete new edition will serve to instruct contemporary students in figure drawing, to present an important nineteenth-century document to historians, and to edify the general art-loving public, collectors, and amateurs.

The plates in the *Drawing Course* are *modèles*, which in English would be translated as "good examples to copy." The course follows the established routine in nineteenth-century art schools by beginning with the copying of plaster casts, proceeding to master drawings, and finishing with nude male models (*académies*). Since this tripartite division of activities was taken for granted in the curricula of the time, the plates were issued without instructions. Relying on the expertise of contemporary teachers and practitioners of academic figure drawing, the present editors have tried to indicate how these plates might be taught in classes and used by individual students today. Throughout, every attempt has been made to explain nineteenth-century drawing theory and practice.

The present book also introduces the figure of Charles Bargue (1826/27–1883), a lithographer and painter known now only to a small group of connoisseurs, collectors, and art students. An attempt has been made to clear his life of legend and to write a biography based upon the scant surviving evidence. His painted œuvre is small, and only about fifty titles have been recorded. Of those, only half have been located, most of which are in private collections. His *Drawing Course* is known to only a few through stray and scattered surviving sheets and from the hitherto only known complete set of the *Drawing Course* in the National Art Library, Victoria and Albert Museum, London. In 1991 two further complete sets were made public as a result of the founding of the Musée Goupil in Bordeaux. The plates reproduced in this book were selected from these two sets.[2] To make the introduction to Bargue more complete, an illustrated and annotated listing of all his known paintings has been included as well.

The first two sections of the *Drawing Course* were intended for use in the French schools of design, or commercial and decorative art schools. It was believed that in order to produce articles of commerce and industry that could compete on the international market, designers of utilitarian objects would benefit from knowing the guiding principles of good taste. (This was the argument in the brochure issued by Goupil & Cie to advertise the course *On Models for Drawing* [*Des modèles de dessin*]; see appendix 1 for an English translation of the text). Good taste, or *le grand goût*, was based on classical form, which was defined by the rarefied style of antique statuary. The combination of good taste and the study of nature resulted in *le beau idéal*—the rendering of nature in its most perfect manifestation—sometimes referred to more specifically as *la belle nature*.

The third section on drawing after live models, by contrast, was issued for use in art academies. Drawing after live models was discouraged or even prohibited in European and American schools of design, that is, in schools of commercial or applied arts, and was only seldom and reluctantly included in their curricula; it was strongly felt in the artistic establishment that commercial artists should not be encouraged to develop aspirations or pretensions beyond their perceived abilities.[1] The *académies* of the third part are examples of how the Neoclassicism of the early-nineteenth-century academy was revised by the new interests of the Realist movement. The Realists did not generalize their figures; personal traits—even ugly ones—are observed and recorded. Bargue's presentation of the male nude, although realistic, is always graceful and often noble.

The course sold well for at least three decades, including several large printings for various institutions in England as well as France. Individual plates were still sold by Goupil & Cie and its various successors until the dissolution of the firm in 1911. The lithographs were evidently worn out by use; some older art schools still have a few surviving relics of the set, usually framed and hung on the studio walls as examples of nineteenth-century assiduity.

The teaching of traditional academic practices almost died out between 1880 and 1950, as the number of academically trained instructors gradually diminished. This decline was concurrent with a shift in emphasis from an objective imitation of nature to a subjective reaction to the world, or even to the abstract qualities of art itself. This was a major revolution in art theory. Since antiquity Aristotle's definition of art as mimesis, or the imitation of nature, had dominated Western thought and practice. Before the 1880s "expression" meant the emotion or meaning conveyed by the subject—the person or thing depicted—not the emotional state of the artist, as in today's "self-expression."

The *Drawing Course* reveals what the last generations of traditionally trained representational artists were taught to copy and admire. Scholars investigating artists trained between the Franco-Prussian War and World War I will find that this book helps them understand the training and early work of their subjects. It is well known, for example, that Vincent van Gogh worked independently through the course more than once,[2] and that Picasso copied Bargue plates at the Barcelona Academy.[3] Many early drawings by artists of this generation thought to be drawn from life may, in fact, be copies after the models in the Bargue-Gérôme *Drawing Course*.

Today most art schools have dispensed with teaching drawing after plaster casts as an integral part of learning how to draw; and the modern life class differs greatly from the academic life class. Whereas the earlier training emphasized accuracy, solidity, and finish, modern instruction emphasizes gesture and self-expression, which often results in a nonacademic exaggeration of forms. Earlier the model held one pose for many hours, even weeks; modern life-drawing poses are very short; an hour is considered in many studios to be a long pose.

Many modern teachers and practitioners believe high finish is mechanical and inimical to self-expression. Furthermore, the modern teaching of anatomy is cursory. Modern drawing classes neglect the organic structure and unity of the model.[4] Students in drawing classes are allowed to draw approximate sections of bodies and to accept multiple test lines and accidents without correcting or erasing them. A persistent modern view holds that there are no mistakes in a work of art. The only criterion is the artist's intention.

By contrast, a good academic drawing—today as in the nineteenth century—should be accurate and finished, concerned with organic unity, and devoid of superfluous details. Careful academic practices not only develop patience but also train the student to see mistakes and correct them. In addition, academic theory urges the student to make continuous reference to nature in order to avoid excessive personal expression or mannerisms (maniera). The human figure is viewed and painted with respect, without detachment or a sardonic air of superiority on the part of the artist. The academic tradition exalts the human body.

Public Controversy Over Teaching Materials

The catalyst of the Bargue-Gérôme Drawing Course was an official controversy about how best to teach drawing to French students of design and industry. A Parisian exhibition of student work in 1865 by the Central Union of Applied Arts (Union centrale des Beaux-Arts appliqués) caused much consternation. Eight thousand drawings and sculptures by students from the art departments of 239 public educational institutions had been put on display; officials and critics were united in decrying the exhibits as very poor in quality. Since early drawing education in the industrial and decorative art schools consisted mainly of copying after prints or casts, the general conclusion was that they had been given poor models.

At the exhibition's awards ceremony the sculptor Eugène Guillaume (1822–1905), director of the École des Beaux-Arts, verbalized his colleagues' dissatisfaction: "The main ingredient of art is taste. On this account, we are afflicted by the weakness of the models that are called upon to develop it. To place before the eyes of beginners in our schools examples devoid of all ennobling sentiments,' to have copied engravings and lithographs of a false style, of incorrect drawing, of schematic method—this amounts to the corruption of the taste of the nation; it makes the development of vocations impossible. These fundamentals of [art] instruction must be rigorously reformed."[5]

Ernest Chesneau (1833–1890), an art critic who became an inspector of fine arts in 1869, delved further into the problem in a series of articles published in Le Consitutionnel. Although he, too, expressed his unhappiness and dissatisfaction with the works on display, he saw a silver lining:

> [T]he great benefit of this exhibition will be its having opened the most obstinately closed eyes; of forcing the opinion of a few to become the general opinion; of leading, we hope, to a complete reorganization of the teaching of drawing. A reform as radical as this, I can't deny, is very difficult to achieve, but it has become absolutely necessary after the lamentable spectacle that offered us—under the pretext of drawing—a run of over a thousand meters . . . of everything that black and white together could create of inept, ridiculous, and poverty-stricken forms, deprived, with practically no exceptions, not only of any of the feelings of art but also distant from any resemblance, from any shadow of the foundations of the science of drawing: accuracy, life, beauty. . . . The lack of models! that is the dominant cry among the complaints provoked by the examination of the exhibition. . . ."

As an official reaction to the complaints of Guillaume, Chesneau, and others, the Ministre de l'Éducation Publique formed a committee to review available models.

Goupil Proposes a Solution

The demand for better models presented an opportunity that the publishing house of Goupil & Cie could not ignore. In 1868 it published a handsome twelve-page brochure in small quarto entitled On Models for Drawing (Des modèles de dessin). With the self-righteous tone of an official government proclamation, the brochure pompously advertised the Bargue-Gérôme Drawing Course, which was already in print, more than half the plates having been released:

> All the known models and pattern books were passed in review [by a commission specifically appointed for this purpose]; but these models, for the most part, were exactly those that M. Guillaume had just denounced as corrupters of taste. . . .
> Thus it was left to individual initiative to solve the problem. Men of taste and learning applied themselves and a certain number of good models have been published. . . . The Maison Goupil could not remain a stranger to an effort having as its object the response to such a high degree of contemporary concern; it, too, set to work, and with the aid of some practical men it has designed a program whose execution has been entrusted to some distinguished artists. . . .
> Monsieur Charles Bargue, with the association of Monsieur Gérôme, Member of the Institute, was put in charge of the models for drawing the figure.
> In the choice and execution of these models no concessions were made to the pretty[10] or to the pleasant; their severity will doubtlessly discourage false vocations; they will certainly repulse those who think of drawing as an accessory study, a pleasant pastime; thus, it is not to such students that these are offered, but to those who seriously wish to be artists.[11]

The Drawing Course was not unique; there were many others on the market.[12] Around 1860, for example, Bernard-Romain Julien (1802–1871) had published his own course.[13] It was designed for use in the public schools of France, a fact it proudly declared on the title page. It parallels the Bargue-Gérôme course by beginning with details of the face and proceeding to full views of antique statuary. The plates are in a refined, linear, Neoclassical style, yet they might have been the very models against which Chesneau and the committee had reacted. It is hard to see the beautiful Julien plates as "debased," but their elaborately stylized refinement might have made them impractical models for the teaching of basic drawing skills.

Julien's drawing of a head, possibly a Diana (fig. 1), would be bewildering to a beginning student, and the schematic view to the right would not be very helpful. The delineation of the profile between the forehead and nose is subtle, with almost invisible modulations. The hair is complex and would discourage a novice. Furthermore, the dexterous cross-hatching could only be achieved with years of practice. The frontal, diffused lighting supports the clarity of the Neoclassical style but offers no indication of the underlying structure of the head, something needed by students with little experience of anatomy. Bargue, on the other hand, offered clues on how to manage the essential forms of the head and espoused a method to make long, modulated lines easier to manage by abstracting complicated curvilinear outlines into straight lines and angles.

Another Julien plate (fig. 2) depicts the head of the Roman empress Faustina, after a cast also used by Bargue, albeit viewed from another angle (plate I, 43). The Julien drawing omits the back of the head. The lack of a complete outline could lead to errors in the placement of the interior

Fig. 1.
B.-R. Julien. *Classical
Head. (Tête classique.)*
Lithograph. 47 x 28 cm.
(18.5 x 11 in.)

Fig. 2.
B.-R. Julien. *Faustina. (Faustine.)* Lithograph.
47 x 28 cm. (18.5 x 11 in.)

features. (Bargue depicts the entire cast first as a simple outline of points, lines, and angles, making it something measurable.) Julien has drawn the profile of the nose with a straight line, and the hair has been reduced to the demarcation of simplified shadows, with just a few lines. Bargue profits from direct, focused overhead lighting, giving a sense of presence to the figure and revealing the sitter's age. Julien's penchant for frontal lighting underplays the structure and character of his models.

A direct comparison of the *Homer (Homère)* by Julien[14] (fig. 3) and the one by Bargue (fig. 4) more clearly reveals the different approaches of the two courses. In both the drawing is excellent, tight and accurate. However, the proliferation of hatching in Julien's example confuses the relationships of the various volumes of the face. Bargue works tonally, logically progressing from light to dark. The result is a greater range of value from black to white, providing more drama, unity, and volume. It's almost as if Julien were emphasizing the decorative aspects of the antique bust as opposed to Bargue's stress on the sculptural qualities.

HOMÈRE

ÉTUDES
D'APRÈS L'ANTIQUE
LITHOGRAPHIÉES PAR JULIEN

The Organization
of the *Drawing Course*

In the Goupil catalogue of 1868 the *Drawing Course* was announced as *Models and Selected Works for the Teaching of the Arts of Design and for Their Application to Industry (Modèles et ouvrages spéciaux pour l'enseignement des arts du dessin et pour leur application à l'industrie).* The first part was already in print; the second part, *Models after Masters of All Periods and All Schools (Modèles d'après les maîtres de toutes les époques et de toutes les écoles)* was in progress.

The first part, *Models after Casts (Modèles d'après la bosse),*[11] consisted of seventy plates and was described as "in itself a basic and [systematically] progressive course with the purpose of giving the student the capacity to draw a complete academic figure." The publishers were proud that "hardly had the first plates of the [first part of the] course been finished when the city of Paris ordered a special printing for the city schools, and in England the course was adapted by the numerous [educational] institutions supervised by the South Kensington Museum (now the Victoria and Albert Museum)." In many instances the Bargue-Gérôme course must have replaced the Julien course.

The brochure vaunts the selection of drawings for the second part: "These models were intended to develop in the soul of the students a feeling and taste for the beautiful, through familiarizing them with creations of a pure and noble style as well as with healthy and vigorous transcriptions of nature" (see appendix 1). It would be completed in 1870 as a set of sixty lithographs by Bargue after renowned old and modern masters.

The third part, *Charcoal Exercises in Preparation for Drawing the Male Academic Nude (Exercices au fusain pour préparer à l'étude de l'académie d'après nature),* contained sixty plates and was completed in 1873. It was not mentioned in the brochure of 1868, and when it was published, it had only Bargue's name on the

Fig. 3.
B.-R. Julien. *Homer. (Homère.)* Lithograph.
45 x 33 cm. (17.75 x 13 in.)
Bibliothèque nationale, Paris.

16

Fig. 4.
Charles Bargue. *Homer. (Homère.)* Detail of plate I, 54.

frontispiece, without a mention of Gérôme (fig. 5).[16] This was the case because almost all of the subjects are original figure drawings by Bargue. Moreover, as was postulated earlier, the inclusion of drawings of nude males to be copied was a logical step after the first two volumes but presumably was not originally thought of as part of the course. Part III was likely disassociated from the first two volumes since it was intended for use in the fine arts schools instead of industrial and decorative arts schools. Possibly Gérôme's role as a collaborator on the project may have expired after the first two editions, or perhaps Gérôme simply respected Bargue's growing prowess and generously delegated the task to his colleague.

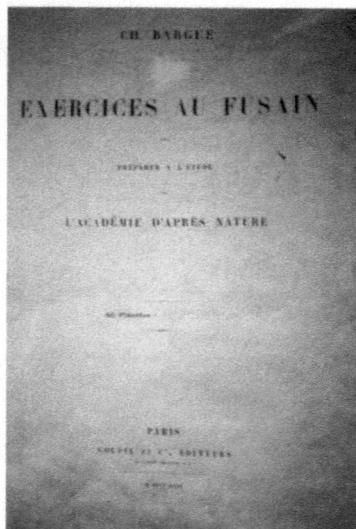

Fig. 5.
Title page of the *Drawing Course,* part III: Chalk Exercises.
(Page de titre du *Cours de dessin.* III: *Exercices au fusain.)*

17

PART I: DRAWING AFTER CASTS
(*MODÈLES D'APRÈS LA BOSSE*)

The first section, *Models after Casts (Modèles d'après la bosse)*, teaches the student how to systematically draw after casts by offering a collection of plates depicting casts of both partial and complete male and female bodies. Most of the casts are after famous ancient sculptures, but a few are taken directly from life.[1] They represent a selection that was duplicated, at least in part, in the collections of most European and American art schools.

There are several advantages to using casts as drawing models. Their immobility permits extended study of a single view or pose; and since they are usually white or painted in a light color, they provide an easier reading of the values of light and shadow on their surfaces. Moreover, the opinion has long persisted that copying casts of ancient sculpture develops good taste. One of the major goals of this course was to teach such elevated taste *(le grand goût)*, the proper selection from among the features and accidents of nature. Antiquity has long held the reputation for having gleaned the ideal human form from among the idiosyncrasies of individual physiognomies and bodies. The resulting classical style was for many centuries almost synonymous with good taste, and its goal was the depiction of *la belle nature*, the representation of natural forms in their purest and most beautiful manifestations, without flaws or accidents.[2] The style is recognized, indeed, defined by clarity, continuity of outline, geometric simplification of shapes, and the rhythmic ordering of forms.

In practice, the classical style sustains the integrity of each individual part of a form while containing the part in a larger, unified whole. The Greek temple facade, for example, presents a unified composition in which the parts are clearly separable and identifiable: the pediment; the entablature; the columns with their abacus, capital, shaft, and base; and the platform. Each part is independent in the exactness of its shape and the precision of its finish, yet each element is still a necessary part of a harmonious whole—that is, taken together they form a column that, in turn, is a part of the facade. Precision, assurance, clarity of form, the independence and interdependence of the parts: these traits make even a fragment of a Greek statue—a foot, a hand, a head, a limbless torso—an admirable, unified object in itself, while still alluding to the harmony of the lost whole.

Until recently art critics and historians chose the most idealizing period of Greek art as the high point of ancient art and named it the classical period (450–400 B.C.). Even so, the works of the sculptors (Myron, Phidias, Polykleitos) and the major painters of the day (Apollodorus of Athens, Zeuxis of Herakleia, Timanthes and Parrhasios) were known only from descriptions in literary sources and copies. Moreover, the few known copies of the paintings are particularly debased. This choice of one period as representative of ancient art ignores the energetic, inventive, and lengthy stylistic evolution of Greek and Roman sculpture, which expressed a variety of mental and spiritual states over a period spanning more than a thousand years,

maintaining high quality while continuing to use the classical style—which was long past its period of dominance—for certain purposes, such as giving dignity to portrayals of gods or statesmen.[19] For centuries critics ignored the production of preclassical statuary as "primitive," and decried the postclassical production as "decadent." *Le grand goût*, based on the art of the classical period (and of the major masters of the Italian High Renaissance), was thought of as the model for representational art. This classical ideal dominated art theory and teaching until it was challenged by the Realist movement of the mid-nineteenth century. After 1850 a new generation of students caught up in the principles of Realism rebelled against the practice of drawing after casts because they believed the classical conventions practiced in ancient sculpture prevented them from seeing nature accurately. For example, the young American painter Thomas Eakins (1844–1916) was a student in Gérôme's atelier at the École des Beaux-Arts in Paris during the 1860s. The students drew from life and then after casts, alternating every three weeks. Already a stubborn American Realist at eighteen, Eakins stayed home during the weeks devoted to drawing after casts.[20]

Two fine paintings, one by Jean-Auguste-Dominique Ingres entitled *Achilles Receiving the Ambassadors of Agamemnon (Les Ambassadeurs d'Agamemnon)* (fig. 6) and the other by the American master Thomas P. Anshutz, a student of Eakins, entitled *The Ironworkers' Noontime (La Pause de midi des ouvriers métallurgistes)* (fig. 7) clearly demonstrate the differences between the Neoclassicism at the start of the nineteenth century and the Academic Realism of the second half of the century. Both feature a row of masculine bodies—albeit a bit less nude in the Anshutz—all with varied features in assorted traditional studio poses. Ingres sets out a sample set of classical types: the youthful Apollonian hero Achilles; the younger Praxitilian Patrocolus; the slender, Mercurial Ulysses; and the Herculean Ajax. All are adaptations of classical statuary in Rome or Naples, and each represents one of the ages of man (the set is completed by the melancholic, brooding, elderly Briseus in the middle ground and the children playing in the distance).

The poses used by Anshutz are based on common studio poses. The underlying classicism is somewhat disguised by the nonidealized portrait heads, individualized bodies, and the recording of specific accidental traits (such as the sunburn patterns). Whereas Ingres uses a general light with just enough shadowing to model his figures, Anshutz imitates the sunlight of high noon, with resulting strong shadows, which, however, do not distort the forms. Nonetheless, both stick to the classical tradition of a frieze of figures united by their rhythmic placement and movement across the picture plane. Ingres's characters exist in the timeless world of mythology; Anshutz's figures are placed in a specific modern context, a factory yard. Thus, despite their differences, the two paintings are strongly related, demonstrating that Academic Realists retained, albeit latently, many of the interests, habits, and practices of Classicism.

The use of casts in the teaching of drawing gradually diminished until, by the 1920s, it was hardly practiced. By the 1950s even the once strict practice of drawing after live models had become merely a freehand event, without direction or criticism, and certainly without system or method.[21] The result was a decline in the quality of objective painting even by artists who wanted to maintain traditional standards.

Throughout the twentieth century the grand cast collections in the academies and art schools, which had been assembled with such effort and cost for over a century, were sold, given away, destroyed, or left to languish in corridors, subject to student pranks and mutilation.

Against the history of these changes, the Bargue-Gérôme *Drawing Course* can be seen as an attempt to balance contemporary Realism with the practices of classical Idealism. The authors intended to teach a method of drawing the human figure from nature with *good taste*, to instill in their students a practice based on careful selection, simplification, and a knowledge of the structure of the human figure. The method taught was newly informed with the excitement of the

Fig. 7.
Thomas Anshutz. *The Ironworkers'
Noontime. (La Pause de midi des ouvriers
métallurgistes.)* 1880-81. Oil on canvas.
43.3 x 61 cm. (17 x 24 in.)
Fine Arts Museums of San Francisco. (Gift
of Mr. and Mrs. John D. Rockefeller 3rd,
1979.7.4)

Realist movement of the mid-nineteenth century, and for a while—even against the incoming tide of modernism—the combination supported the creation of great modern history and genre paintings.[7]

The abandonment of the study of the classical ideal in the last quarter of the nineteenth century was a serious break in an established yet vital artistic tradition. After all, Western art is an artificial activity that became self-conscious in antiquity and again in the Italian Renaissance, each time articulating an intellectual, apologetic theory of art that continued to influence the creation and teaching of painting over the centuries. The twentieth-century break in this developed tradition is problematic for young, contemporary artists who may not be attracted by the many schools and movements of modernism but are instead drawn to the imitation of nature. Without access to the rich lore and methods of humanist figure painting, they find themselves untrained and underequipped for many of the technical problems that confront them as Realists. Without help, today's young Realist artists may end up uncritically copying superficial appearances, randomly selecting from nature, and unwittingly producing clumsy and incoherent figures.

21

Practical Matters: Using the Plates as Models to Copy

The Schemata or Plans

Most of the plates in part I of the Bargue-Gérôme *Drawing Course* contain two images: a finished drawing of a cast beside a linear schema. The schema, usually to the left, is a guide on how to accurately simplify the optical contour *(mise en trait)* of the cast next to it before starting on the actual depiction of the cast. The schema suggests a useful set of reference lines and sometimes a geometric configuration, around which it would be easy to organize the contours of one's own drawing (see, for example, the triangle drawn around and through the foot in plate I, 5). (The diagrams themselves should not be copied exactly but should be used as guides on how to begin a drawing.) Furthermore, the course presents only generalized rules on procedure; there seems to be no basic underlying formula. However, you should develop a working procedure of your own with reference to examples provided by the course. At the end of part I, when copying the last highly finished plates without a model schemata, you will have to rely on the experience gained from drawing the earlier examples.

The actual drawings after casts were probably done by several—even many—artists from Gérôme's circle of students and friends. We know the name of just one, Lecomte du Nouÿ (1842–1923; see "The Drawing Course" section of the Bargue biography in the present study), and we can safely venture the name of another, Hippolyte Flandrin (1809–1864; see comment to plate I, 70). Bargue copied their drawings on stone for printing as lithographs. The accompanying schemata all exhibit the same penchant for the use of angles, clarity in execution, and simplification of contours; it seems safe to assume that Bargue drew the schemata for the drawings as he copied the finished models on stone; they represent the unifying method of part I. However, there are a few plates where the schemata are less clear (for instance, plate I, 42) and schematized without a specific underlying method. The eyes in plate I, 1, for instance, are not organized around an unvarying point where the plumb line and the horizontal cross each other—say, the pupil—or the inner corner of the eye; instead the crossing point seems to have been chosen at random. In contrast, the other Bargue schemata are clear in purpose, skillfully organized, and based on carefully chosen angle points.

This chapter introduces and defines some terms that will be used in describing a systematic procedure for copying the model drawings. There are, of course, other methods, and if you are copying the Bargue drawings under supervision, the teacher or drawing master may suggest alternative procedures.

Start with the first drawing, work your way through the rest in sequence, or skip ahead judiciously based on your increased skill or the permission of your instructor. You will quickly note that each subdivision of part I ends with a challenging, highly finished drawing; the section on legs, for instance, ends with the fully modeled drawing of the legs of Michelangelo's *Dying Slave* (plate I, 30).

You will soon come to appreciate the skill that produced these plates, as well as their exceptional refinement. Even if you do not understand what you are copying, continue to work with accuracy. Sometimes you will not know exactly what a line or a shadow describes until you have correctly rendered it. By grasping Bargue's achievement, you will raise your own power of observation and simplification.

Materials

The lithographs were made after charcoal drawings and were intended to be copied in charcoal. You should use this medium if you have adequate command of the technique. Use natural kiln-dried vine charcoal in sticks, and reserve charcoal pencils for finishing (the binder used in them makes their lines difficult to erase). Only charcoal can equal the intensity of the blacks in the reproductions, and vine charcoal erases easily. However, you should not use it as a beginner without instruction; the use of charcoal presents too many difficulties to solve by yourself.

If you are a beginner, or if you prefer pencil, you should have a selection of well-sharpened grades—2H through B2 (remember that pencils softer than HB are difficult to use without producing slick, shiny surfaces)—and a good, kneadable eraser. Pencil cannot achieve the same density of darkness as in the plates. Any attempt to produce similar shadows with pencil will result in a multitude of loose flecks of carbon that will repeatedly spoil other areas of your drawing. Strive instead for overall lighter shadows and relatively lighter halftones.

Some of the more detailed plates need to be enlarged before you can copy them. Use a good color laser printer to have them magnified two or three times. The original plate size is 60 x 46 centimeters (24 x 18 inches). In their present size, you might not be able to see or copy many of the fine details, especially if you are working in charcoal. Regardless of the drawing medium used, you need high-grade, well-sized paper with a slight tooth and a surface that can take much erasure. Seek the advice of your art-supply dealer or artists you know. Inferior materials will lead to frustration and keep you from finishing the drawing accurately and neatly.

Drawing Terms

A *point* is a dot or mark without dimensions on a drawing surface. A *line* is a mark generated by extending a point (dot) between two points on a flat surface. Two lines that intersect or join form an *angle*. Points, lines, and angles constitute the basic elements for constructing the *contour* or *outline (mise en trait)*, the visual outer shape of an object.

Basically, drawing is the act of choosing critical elements from nature and recording them on paper while preserving their relationships. As you study the relationships of points, lines, and angles observed in nature, ask yourself: Is one point higher or lower than the other? Is one line longer or shorter than another? Is one angle more or less acute or obtuse than another? Asking these questions and making such comparisons will enable you to analyze and record the shape of the Bargue cast drawings or of any other object.

One of the goals of the course is to teach you to estimate distances, angles, and relationships with your eye. Some students use a pencil, a knitting needle, a taut piece of string, or a plumb line[23]—held with outstretched, locked arms and one eye closed—in order to more accurately measure the distances between certain points on the model and on their paper. This practice requires that you always look at the drawing or object from exactly the same unvarying position (see appendix 2). Some students also use a ruler or an angle with a protractor, which may save hours of frustration. However, you should train your eye to estimate these distances without recourse to tools.

Suggestions for Copying the Plates

Step 1: Make your drawing the same size as the plate you are using. This will facilitate direct comparison with the model. Then begin each drawing by locating the extreme points on the cast: the highest point, the lowest one, and those to the left and the right. Complex poses with extended arms, feet, and joints may require another dot or two to circumscribe. Make approximate marks for these four points on the paper. When joined by contour lines, they will form an irregular rectangle or shape that contains the basic shape of the cast and fixes the overall proportions. You will develop a more concise contour of the subject within this rectangle by measuring more angle points on the contour of the subject and placing them on the drawing, using your rectangle as a guide.

Step 2: As an organizational tool, draw a vertical reference line (hereafter referred to as a plumb line except in cases where the term might be ambiguous) on the paper by either copying the one from the schema or from the highest point of the cast. This line not only shows how the peak of the cast relates to the lowest point but also reveals how interior points for features inside the outline relate to each other. Since many of your initial calculations will be approximate, the plumb line becomes an invaluable empirical device. Additional vertical reference lines can assist in the understanding and drawing of complex areas.

Step 3: See which interior points the plumb line crosses on the plate and mark them on your drawing. For example, on plate I, 43 (Faustina) *(Faustine)* the plumb line intersects the top of the head and crosses through the left brow and the top of the eye. It then passes closely by the left nostril, conveniently touches the left corner of the mouth, but misses the bottom of the cast. From this line one concludes that the inward corner of the left eye relates directly to the left corner of the mouth. This is the type of observation about internal relationships that one should continually make as the drawing progresses.

Step 4: After establishing the verticals, examine the horizontals. For example, the right extremity of plate I, 43 occurs near the hairline overhanging the projection of the nose. The line drawn horizontally across the brow indicates that the width between the plumb line and the ear on the left is much greater than the distance from the same line to the edge of the right brow. Judge by sight the distances from the central plumb line to other points or angles on the contour and inside the cast; then mark their positions in your drawing. When you are drawing an entire figure and are looking at the head or feet from your standing position, do not move your head up or down, just the eyes. Failure to hold the head steady often results in elongated legs.

Step 5: Your drawing should now resemble plotted points on a graph, locating the heights and widths of the contours and interior features. Observe the angles that would be formed if the lines were connected; then join them with reference to the Bargue schema. Since the junctures of the plumb line and horizontal reference lines form right (ninety-degree) angles, use them to judge the relative degree of other angles. If the angles appear too acute or obtuse, study the finished model and correct them. Break curved lines into a series of two or more straight lines. For example, in plate I, 43 two straight lines describe the upper right brow, but seven straight lines plot the complexities of the ear. The Bargue plates offer many examples of how to abstract a complex contour into straight lines. Occasionally slightly curved lines are used instead of straight ones.

However, almost all curves can be reduced to straight lines that cross at the apex. Breaking up curves into straight lines enables you to ascertain the exact inflection point and amplitude of the curve. When you draw curves unaided, they tend to become arcs. Moreover, when drawing an arc it is hard to know when to stop.

Noting anatomical landmarks can be helpful at the outset in order to accurately draw the outline and establish the proportions. For example, the indentation on the right side of the nose and the pit of the neck are indicated within the outlines on plate I, 43. Likewise marks are made for some interior forms of the ear. These notations will vary from one cast to another. Looking up unfamiliar areas or parts in anatomy books and learning their names will help clarify your thinking.

Step 6: The next step is drawing the boundaries of the shadows. At this point your copy should appear relatively close to the preliminary schema or—if the plate has three steps—the second one. In plate I, 34 (Dante) *(Dante)*, the division between shadow and light is indicated with a line. For the most part, the shadow line is a generalization of the shadow's complex meandering across the cast, so do not make it emphatic. Squinting at the model will help in discovering this dividing line between light and shadow, for it will consolidate the dark masses. So will looking at it in a black mirror.[24] Do not outline the halftones (sometimes referred to as half-tints, from the French *demi-teinte).*

To repeat, begin each cast drawing by determining the most important points and general angles (with the aid of a plumb line or some other tool). Do not attempt to transcribe curves; average them with a series of straight lines. Concentrate on the large forms while ignoring small ones. Continually examine and correct the outline; anticipate the next set of more complex points, straight lines, and angles before attempting any modeling.

Values and Modeling

In art theory and practice, the term *value* refers to the relative lightness or darkness of an area exposed to light (some writers substitute *tone* for *value*). It can also be used to describe the absolute brightness of an object (seen or imagined as being without shadow or reflection on its surface). This even value is sometimes called the *local value* of the object. For example, a gray object has a darker local value than a white one.

In nature, values reveal the geometry of an object in relation to a light source. For instance, each side of a cube will have a different value because each has a different spatial orientation to the light source, a different amount of received light, and—to the viewer—a unique perspective. Similarly, the values will be affected by the kind of light hitting it (direct, diffused, or reflected) and by the strength of that light source (bright or dim). These distinctions all present difficult problems for the artist.

In drawing, the transcription of the relative values of an object is called *modeling*. There are three techniques for modeling: stumping *(estomper)*, veiling *(grainer)*, and hatching *(hacher)*. Stumping is the rubbing of the drawing medium into the paper, usually with the pointed end of a paper tightly rolled into a stick, called a stump *(estompe)*. Due to its cleanliness and precision, the stump is preferable to the fingertip. Stumping produces a soft, atmospheric effect.

The second technique, veiling, involves the drawing of faint lines with the pencil or charcoal tip lightly over the paper's grain. This technique alters the value in a very subtle manner; the effect may appear much like translucent veils or glazes. Veiling is useful when modeling delicate forms in the light and where the curvature is gradual.

Hatching, the third method, is the building up of dark value by means of thin parallel lines; when these lines cross each other at angles, it is called cross-hatching. This is essentially an engraver's technique. Some purists who want all the effects in a drawing to be the product of pure line favor hatching over stumping. Hatching can strengthen the modeling achieved by stumping and veiling. Moreover, hatching adds linear direction when drawn axially and helps to create the illusion of foreshortening when drawn transversely in perspective.

Procedure for Modeling

Step 1: The same rule—work from the general to the specific—applies to modeling as well as to line drawing. Begin with the large, dark, generalized shadow; fill it in evenly while referring to the finished drawing. You may schematize the boundaries in your drawing, but remember that the edge of a shadow is seldom abrupt; still, an area is either in light or in shadow and this difference must be made clear. Once added, shadows give the illusion of sculptural relief.

In modeling the shadows, Bargue downplayed reflected light, which in nature would flood the shadows of an actual white plaster cast. The simple shadows were most likely maintained by using a controlled, direct light and by placing the cast in a shadow box, a three-sided open box, lined with black paper or cloth, which diminishes reflected light (see glossary and section entitled "Excursus: Shadow Boxes" in appendix 2; see also fig. 44.[*])

Shadows record the effects of light and give the illusion of a shape turning in space. A focused light source, with a fairly small aperture (like a spotlight) emphasizes form and casts a shadow that starts out sharp-edged but becomes diffuse as it moves away from the object casting it. A general light, such as that produced outside at noon on a cloudy day, would reduce the shadows to grayish halftones. Classical taste emphasizes clarity of form over showy light effects; as a classicist, Bargue used light to reveal rather than obscure form.

Step 2: After drawing the shadows, analyze the value[*] of the halftones and place them in the drawing. (A halftone is any variant of value between light and dark—say, white and black. There are usually several halftones, of graduated value, in a drawing.) In the early stages of the course, the finished drawings are separated into three values: one for the shadow, another for the halftone area, and the white of the paper for the lights. Both the main halftone area and the shadows are clearly indicated. However, the transition from the halftones to the light areas requires care. Notice that the halftones can appear quite dark next to the lights and be mistaken for shadow. On a scale of values from 1 to 9, where 9 is the value of the paper and 1 is the darkest mark that the pencil or charcoal can make, the halftones on a white cast are around values 5 and 6. The average shadow is around 4, which is a little darker than the value of the halftones.

Step 3: After the darkest, major shadow has been filled in, the halftones are blended into the shadow and gradated toward the light areas. This can be extended to complete the modeling by the recording of every value. Plate I, 56 (Male Torso, back view) *(Torse d'homme, vu de dos)* illustrates the gradual lightening of values from the shadow into the halftones and from the halftones into the light, as well as the delicate transitions within the light itself. Here, too, the halftones and lighter values describe complex forms, as along the border of the scapula and around the dimples near the sacrum. Pay attention to the degree of lightness and darkness represented in the finished cast drawing. Each value relates to the other values yet holds its place within the total effect.

Notice the values of the halftones from area to area along the main shadow. Where the curvature of form is more acute, there are few halftones; a gentle curve produces more. Despite the range of values used in the modeling of the torso, Bargue presented a simplification of values and forms without a confusing proliferation of detail. Such control is a hallmark of the classical style.

Step 4: In general, as the course progresses, the finished drawings grow more complex and contain areas that may appear impossible to copy, especially if you were to work from the plates in the book rather than from enlargements. Resolve a complicated area by analyzing its essential structure. For example, divide the multitudinous curls of a Roman noblewoman into recognizable yet simplified masses or shapes. Squint at the values to obfuscate distractions and to average the values into discernable areas. Get a fresh view by looking at both your drawing and the model in a mirror: backward, upside down, or even sideways. Each step completed will make you aware of the next passage to work on.

Finishing the Drawing

Finish requires time and patience. However, as you gradually become aware of how much you have learned by being careful and accurate, your patience and enthusiasm will increase. Ask for criticism from knowledgeable peers. Study your drawing; it is essential that you learn to see and correct your errors yourself. You could also make a tracing of your drawing and then lay it on top of the plate. Analyze what went wrong, especially if you are working alone. Be strict with yourself. A drawing can be stopped at any time, as long as there are no errors in it.

Remember that the academic artists of the nineteenth century whom you are learning to emulate in this course thought that finish denoted professionalism, that it indicated an orderly mind and represented the complete development of the artist's idea. It was not uncommon for an artist to spend months or even years to complete a work. Accept the fact that classical drawing skills develop slowly and plan to use as much time as needed—hours, days, or even months—to achieve a respectable finish.

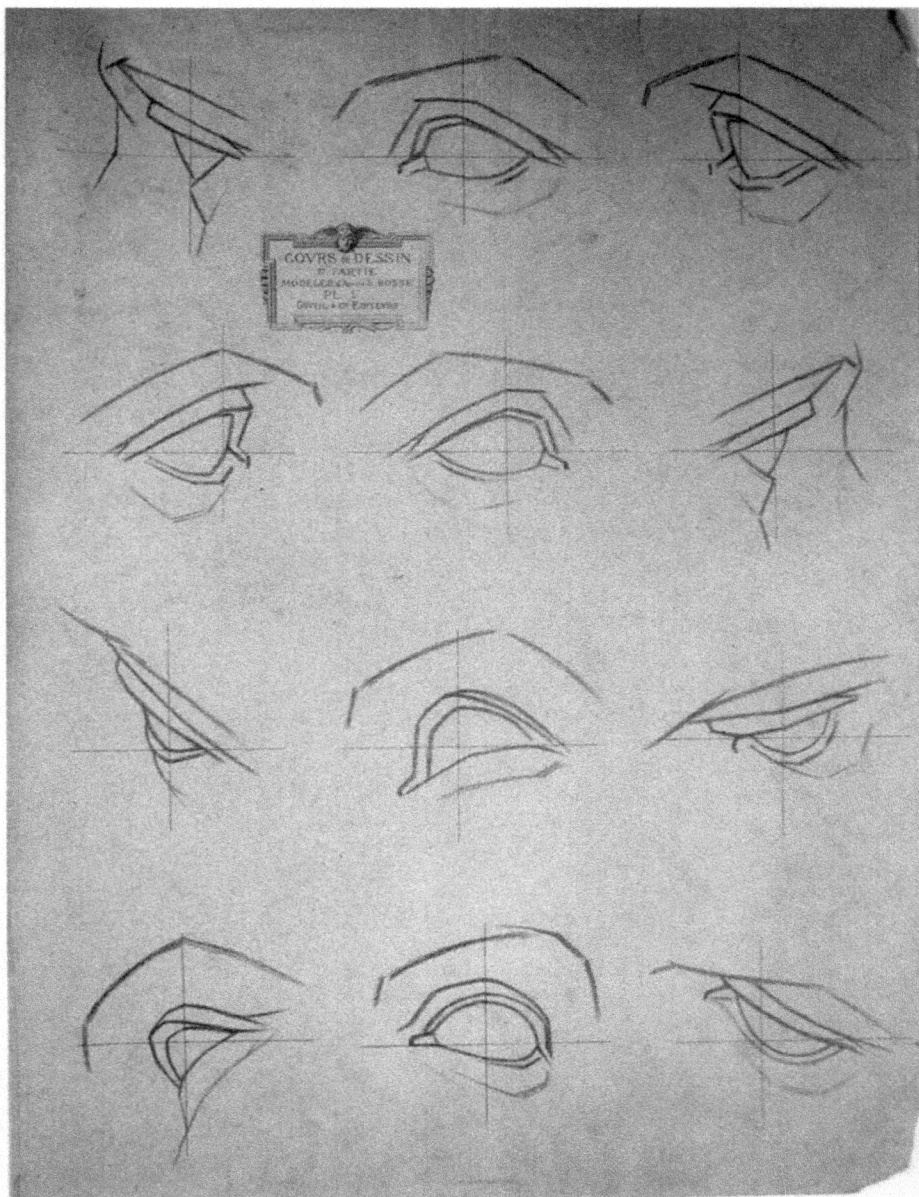

COVRS de DESSIN
1ᵉ PARTIE
MODELES d'après la BOSSE
PL. 5
ONVEIL et EMPERNIE

COVRS de DESSIN
1ᵉ PARTIE
MODELES d'après BOSSE
PL. X
Goupil & Cᵉ Editeurs

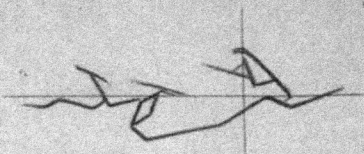

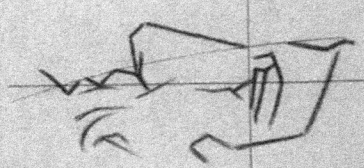

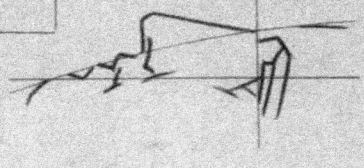

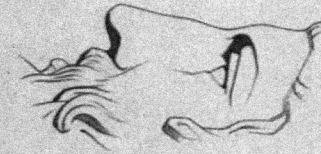

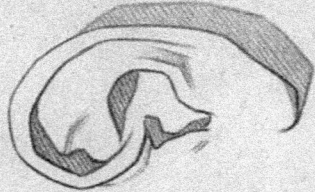

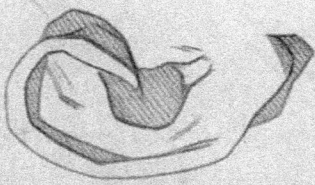

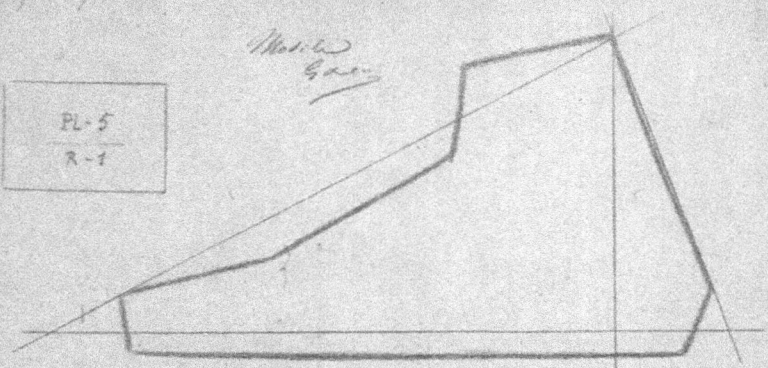

PL·5
R~1

Modelo
Grai

Pl 5   Report 1

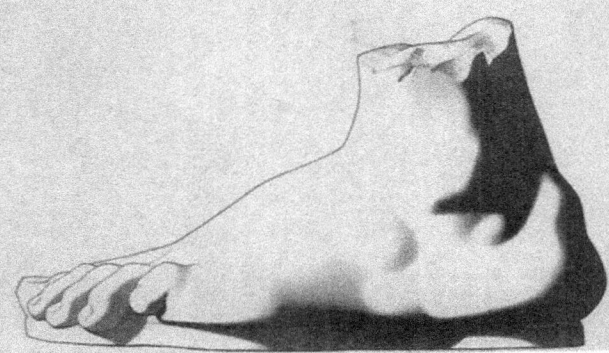

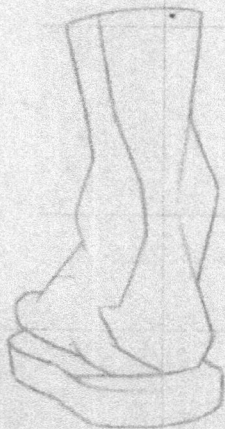

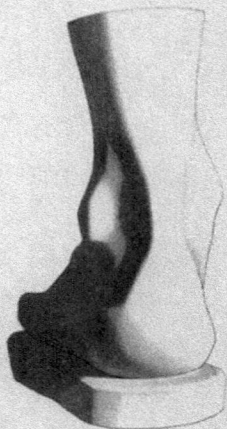

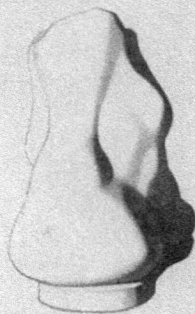

COURS DE DESSIN
1ª PARTIE
MODELE EN PLÂTRE
PL. 6
BOUCHOT EDITEUR

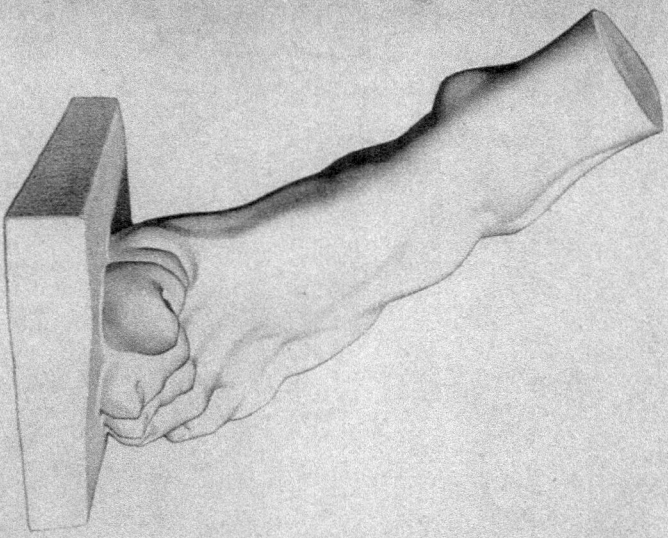

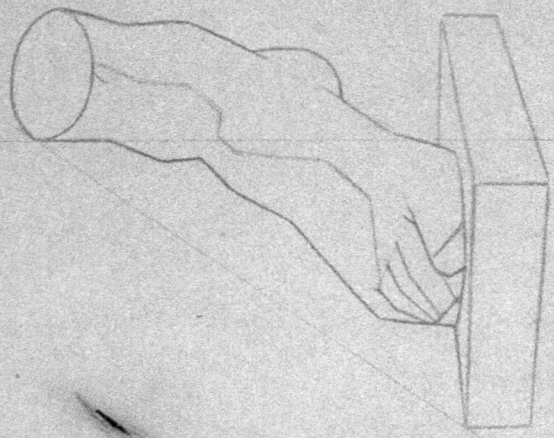

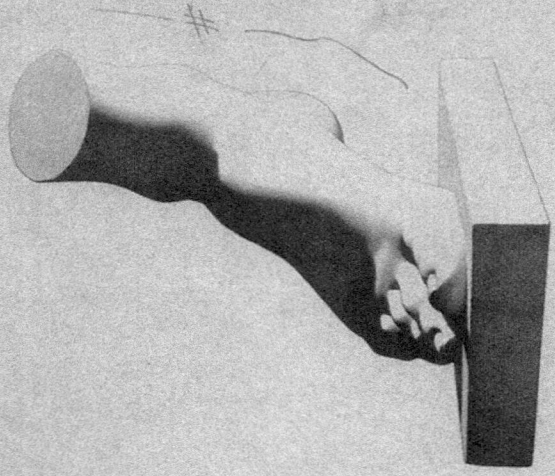

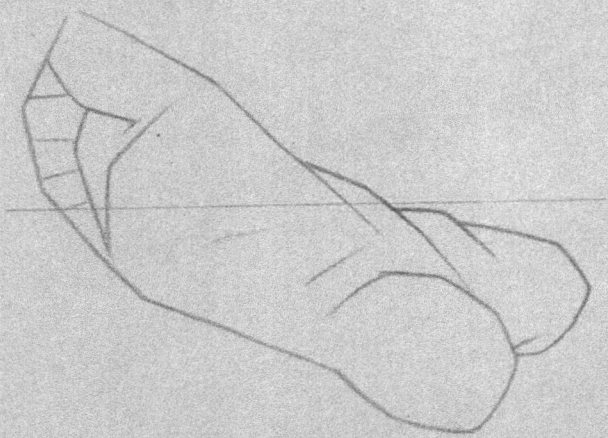

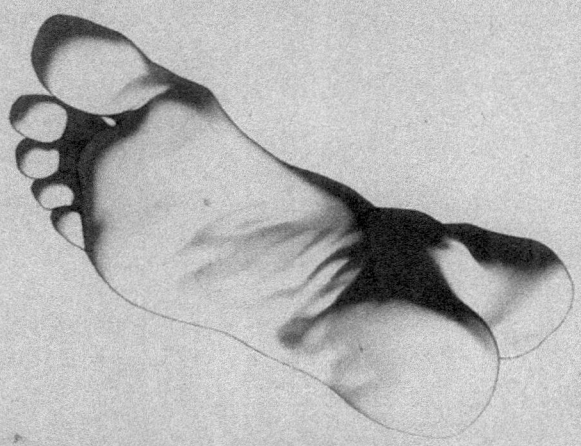

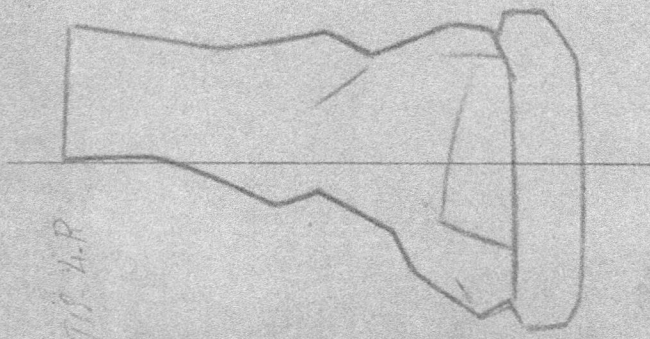

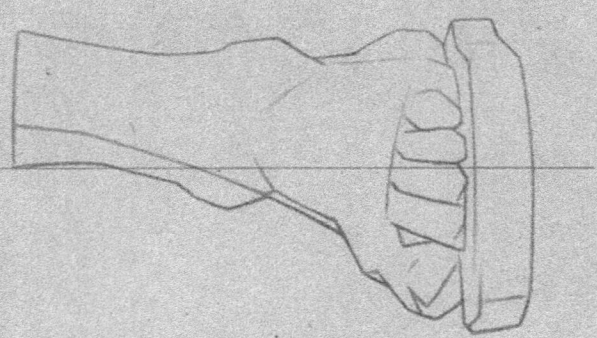

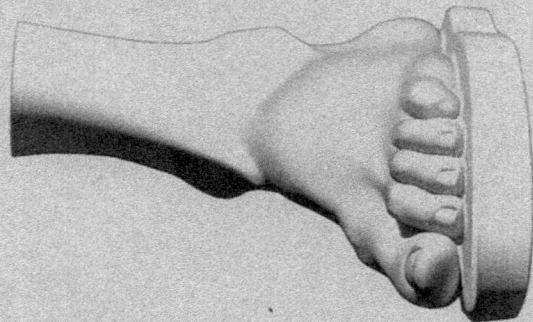

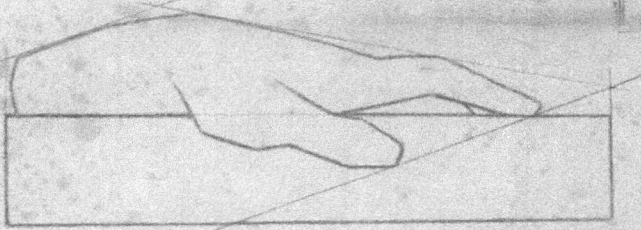

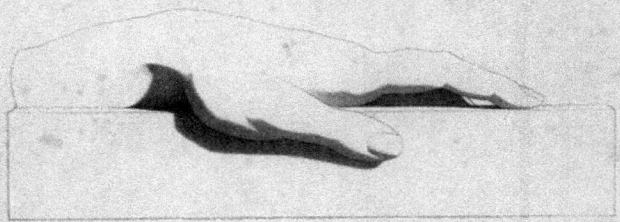

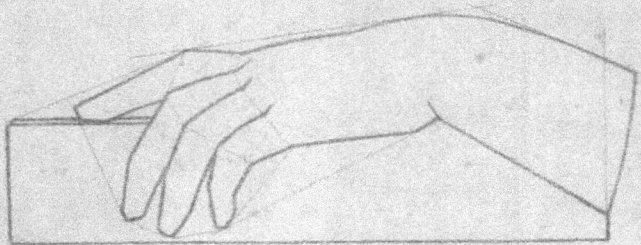

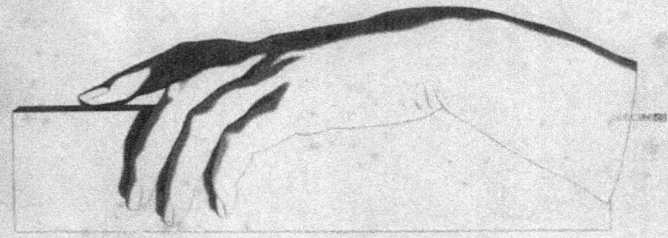

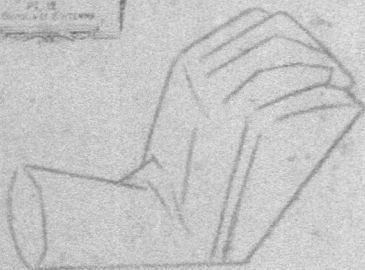
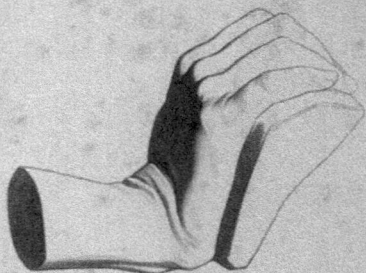

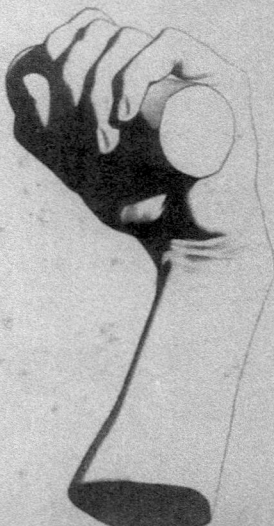

PL- 13   Report N° 1

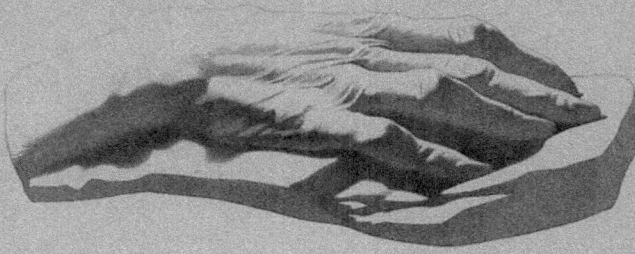

PL-13
R-1

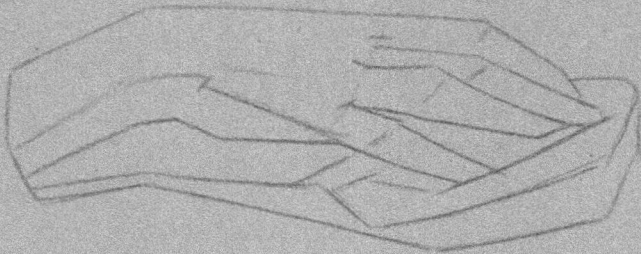

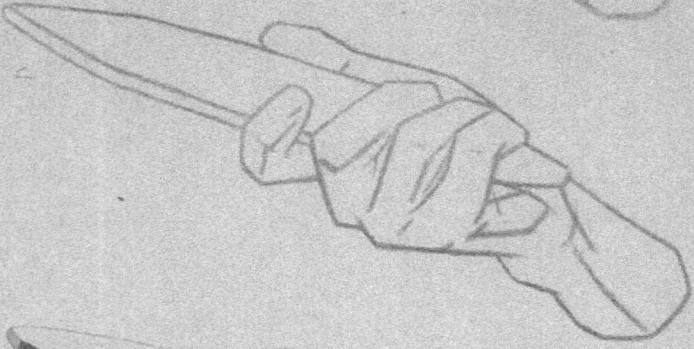

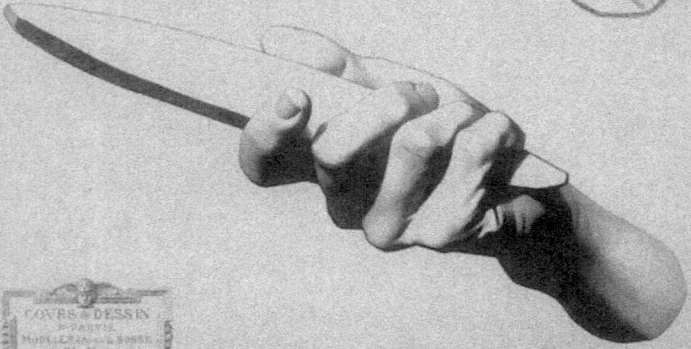

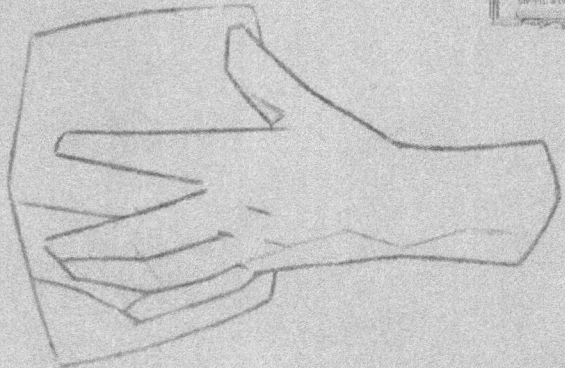

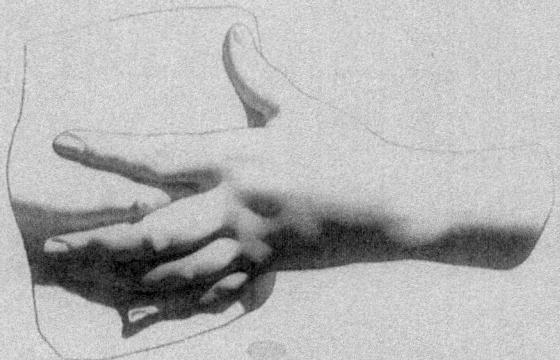

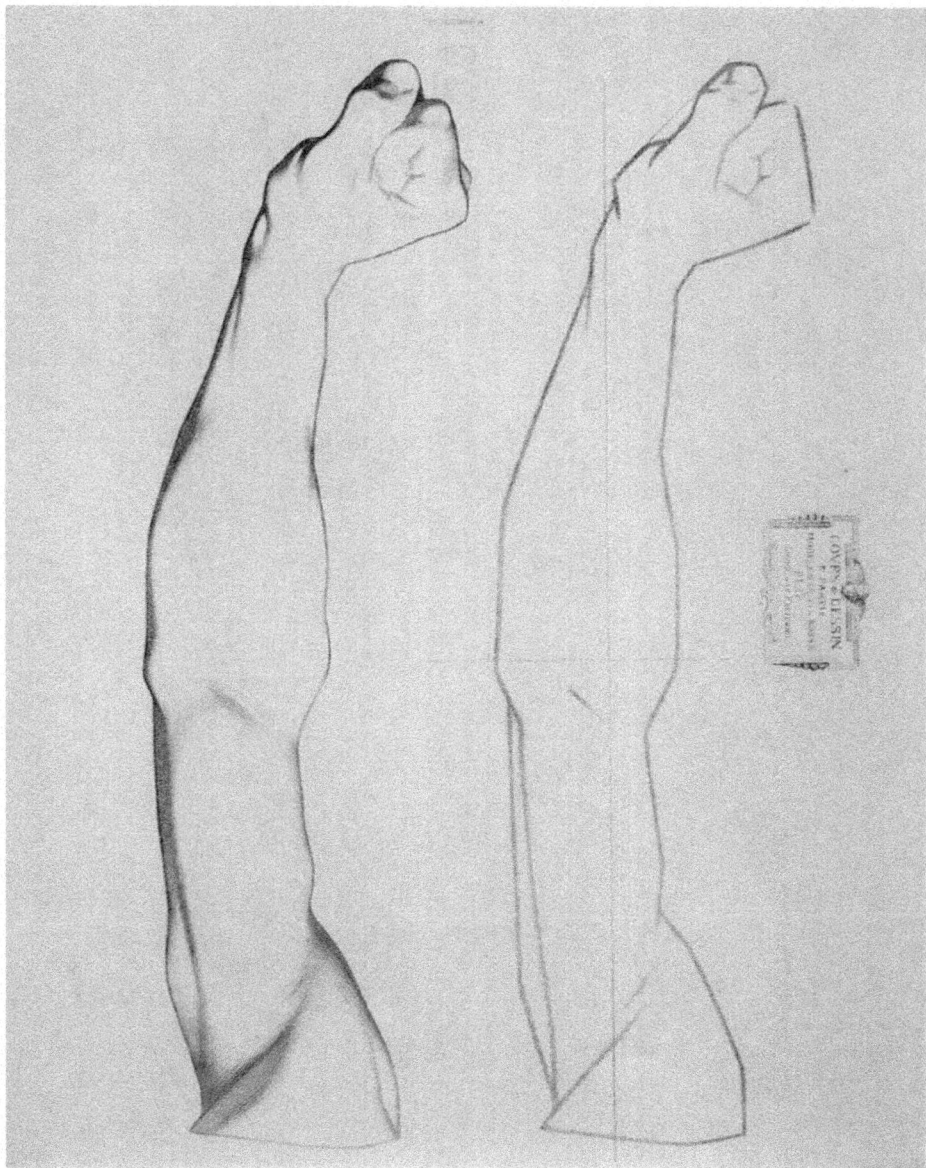

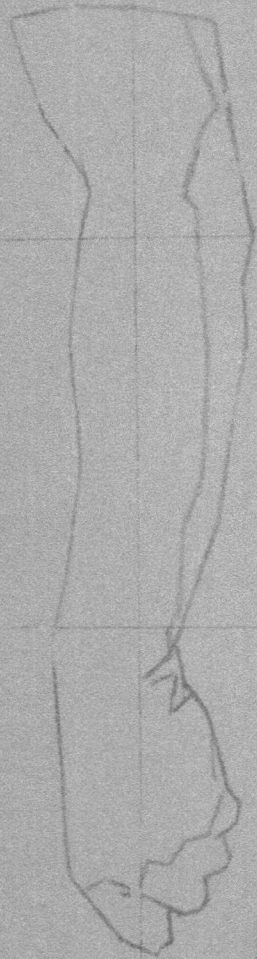

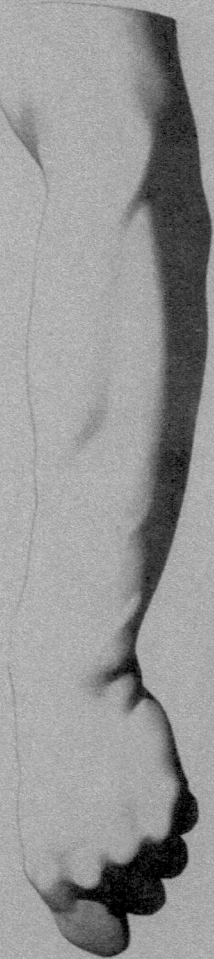

COURS DE DESSIN
2e PARTIE
MORCEAUX DU CORPS
Pl. 11

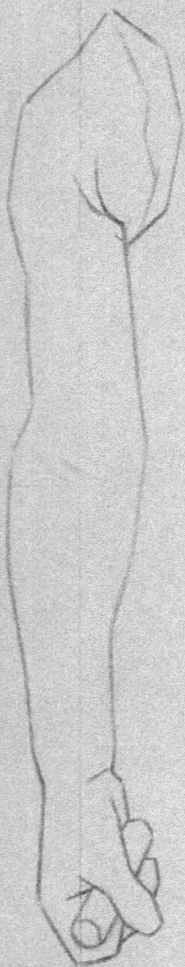

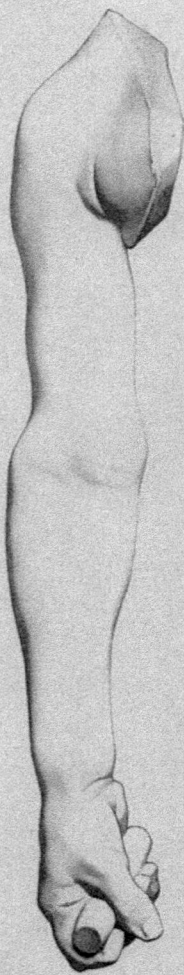

COURS DE DESSIN
2e PARTIE
MODELES D'APRÈS BOSSE
PL. 18
*** & Cie ÉDITEURS

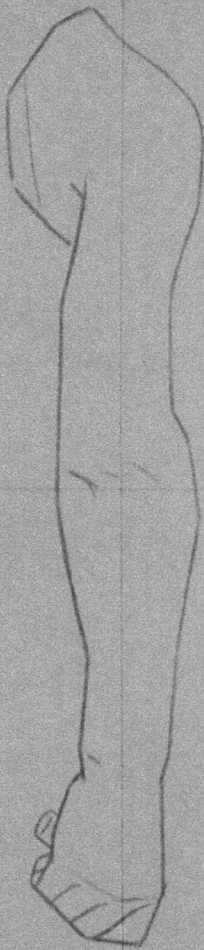

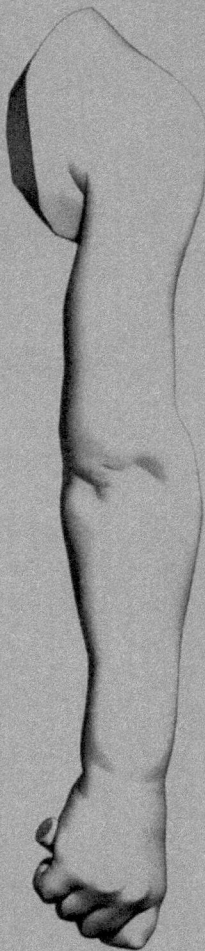

COVRS DE DESSIN
2e PARTIE
MODELES D'APRÈS LA BOSSE
PL. 27
DESSIN D'EN CONTOUR

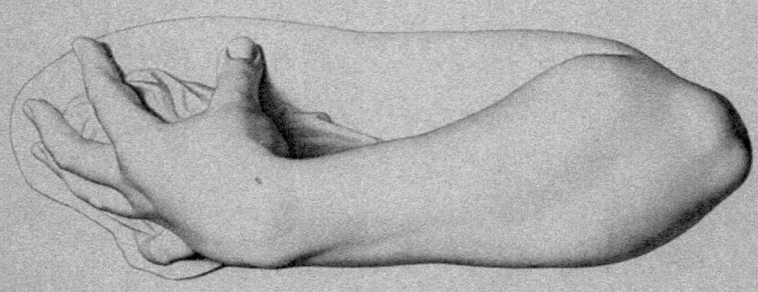

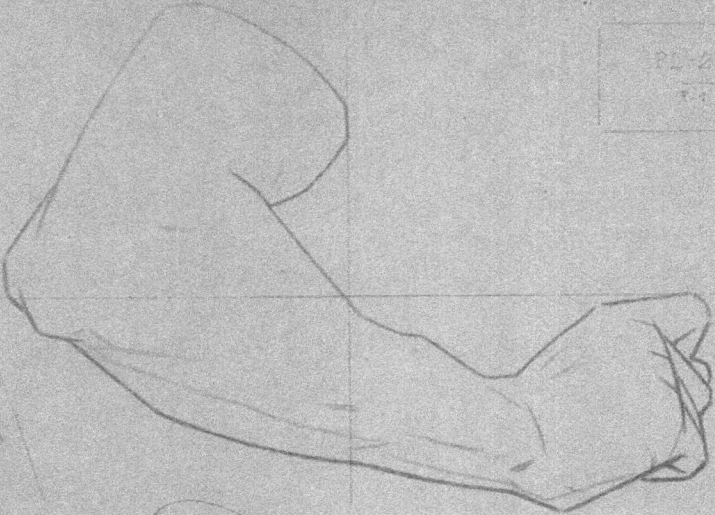

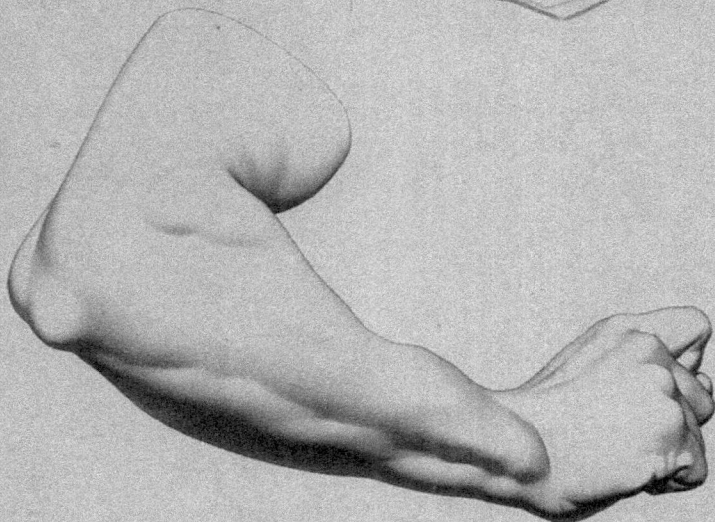

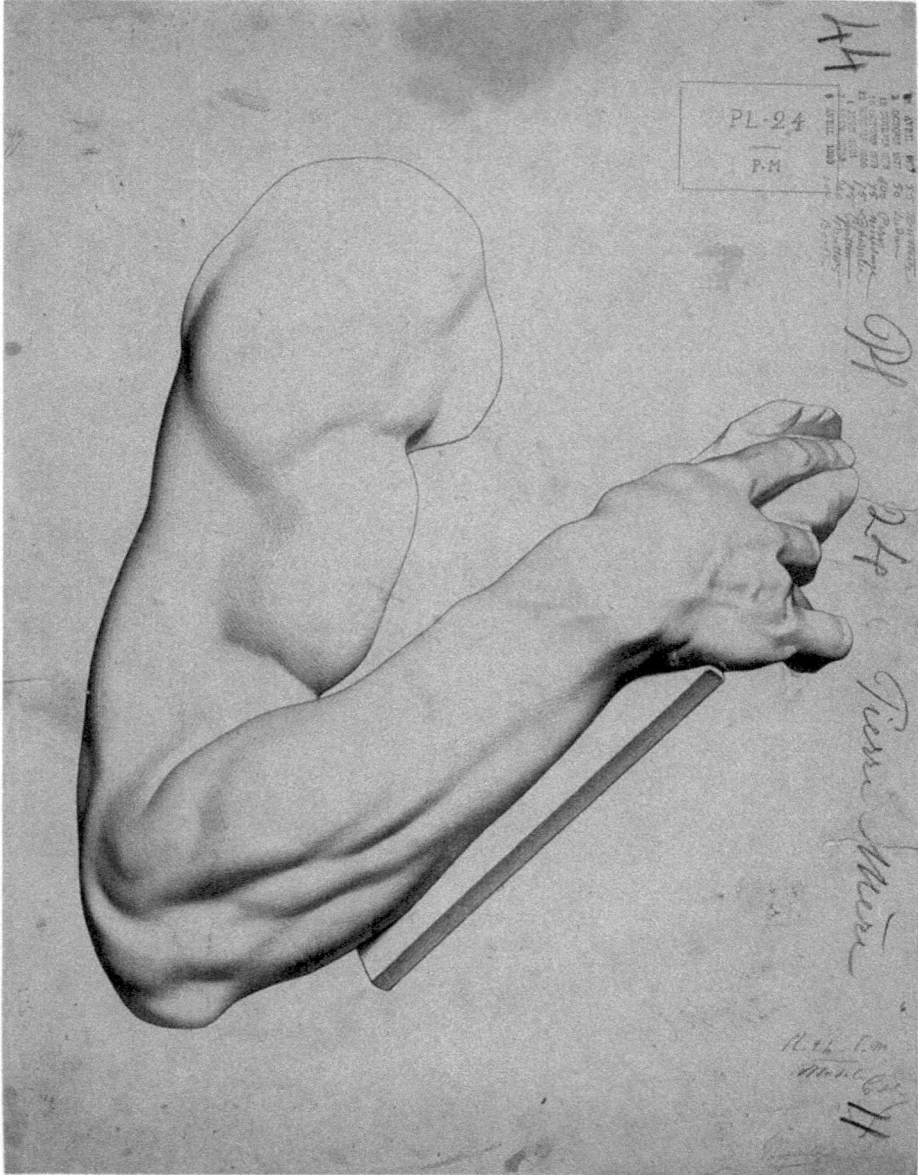

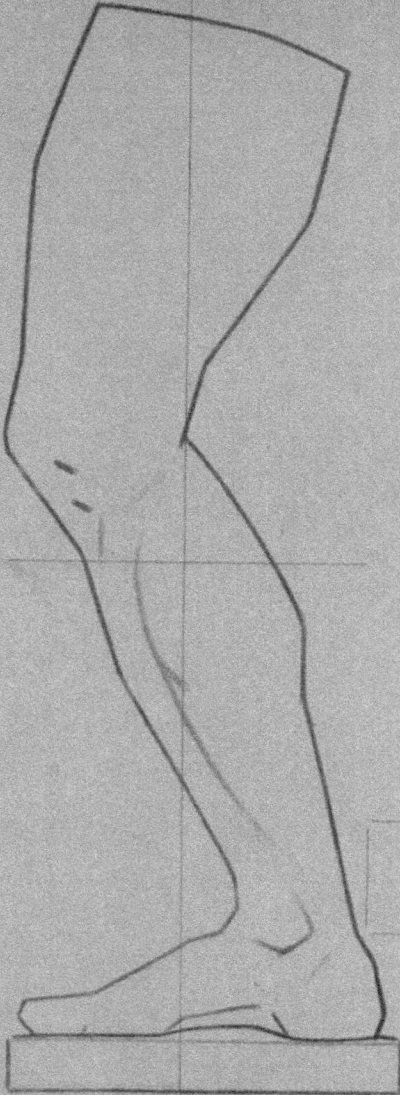

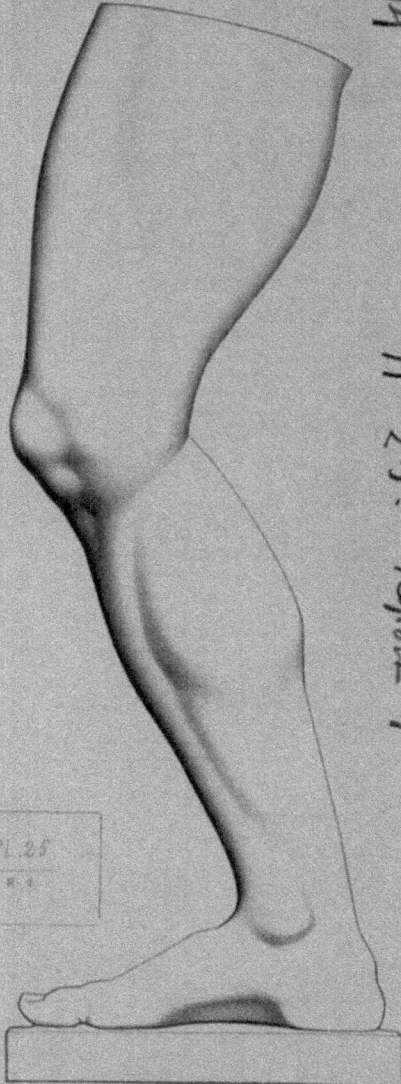

No 25. Report 1

Pl.25

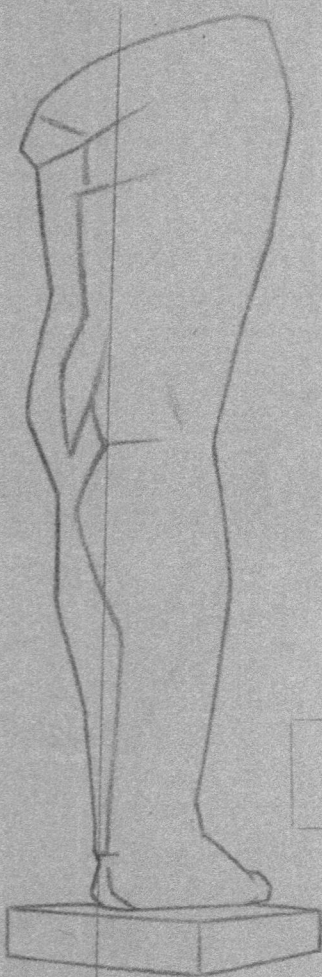 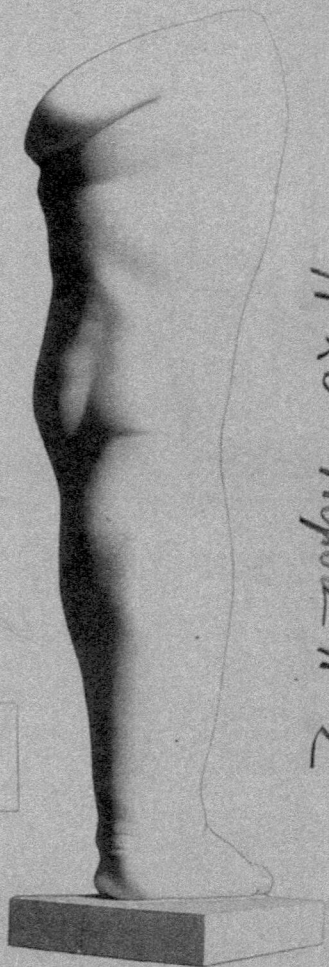

PL-26
—————
R-2

Pl 26 Report N° 2

R. 2 -

71

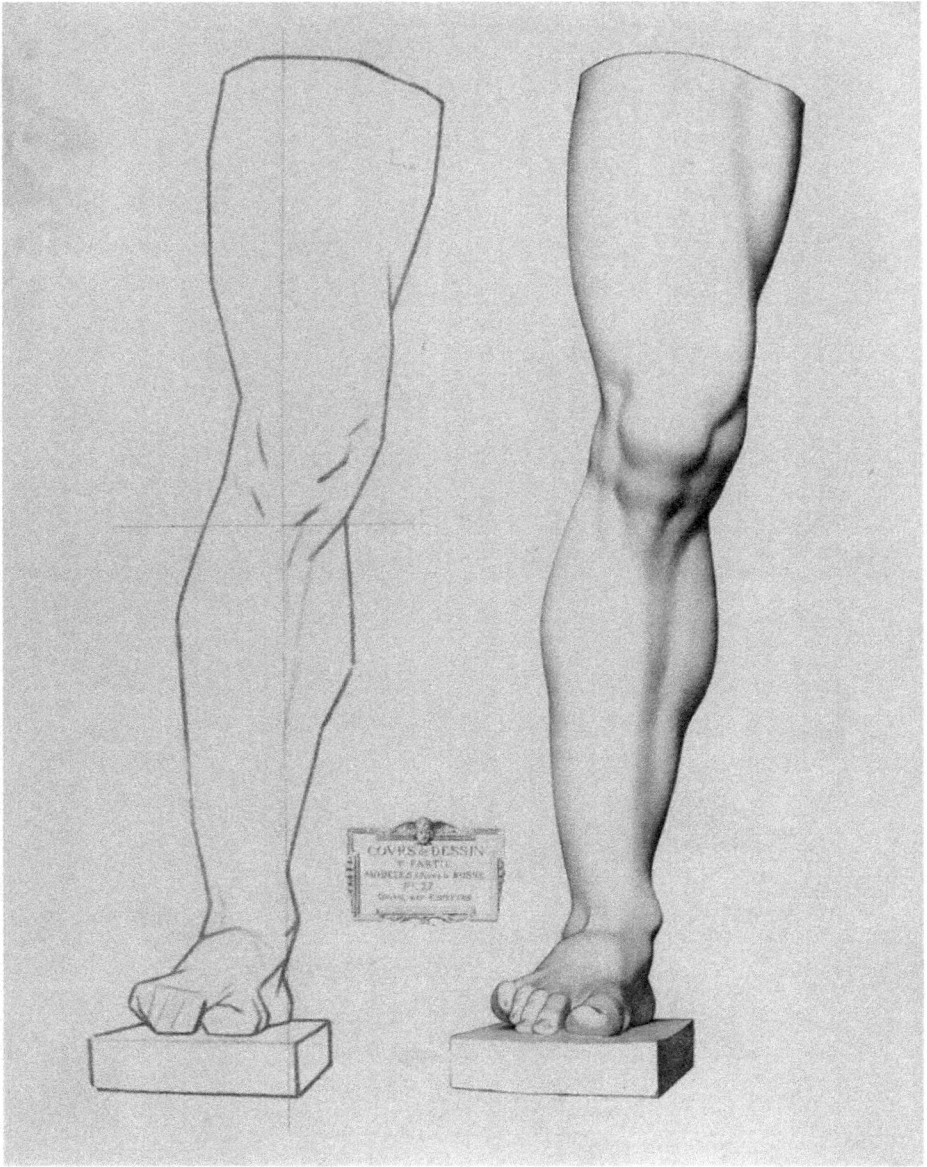

COURS de DESSIN
1re PARTIE
MODÈLES d'après la BOSSE
No 27
GRAND-EMPIRE

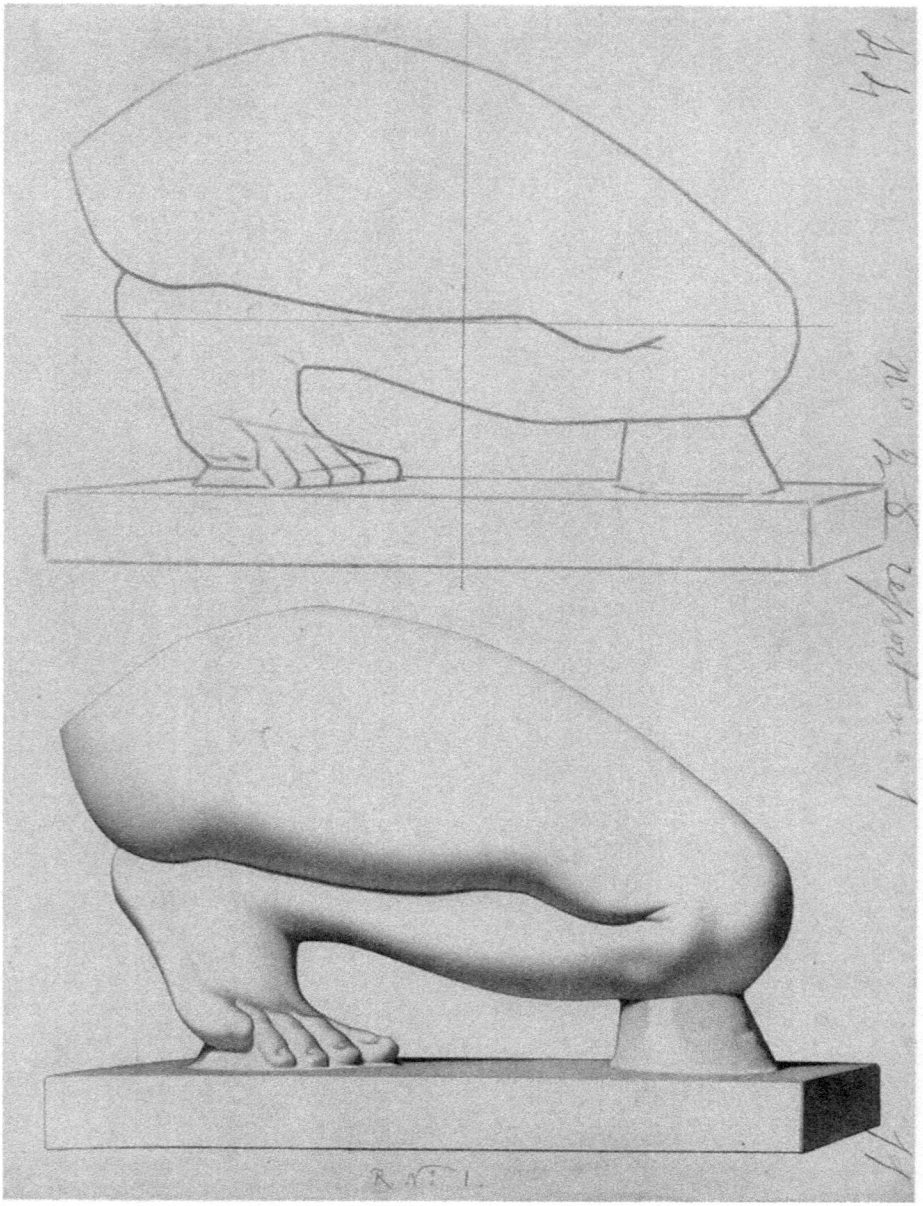

No 8 ziyerleu 8 No 1

11

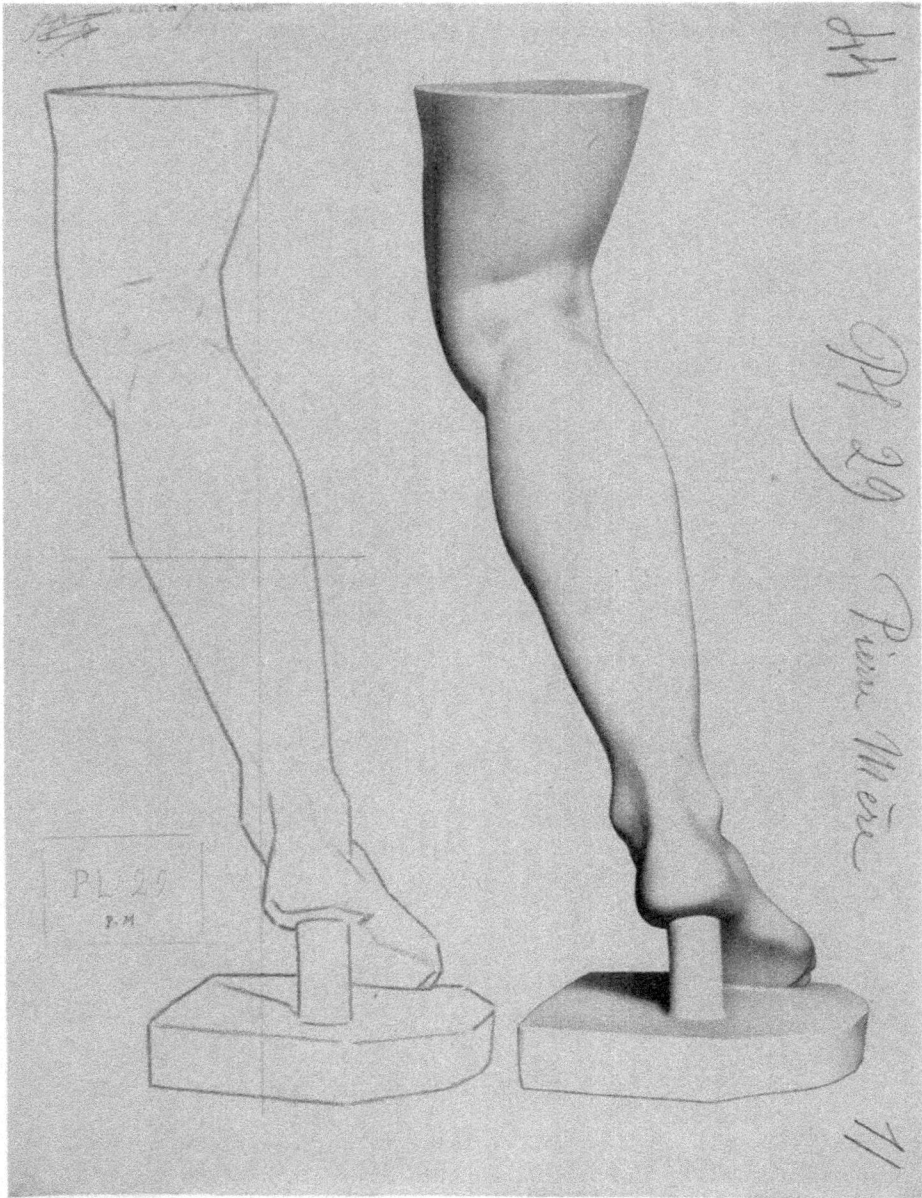

Pl. 29 Pied Méd.

PL. 29
P. M.

IL CARDINAL XIMENES

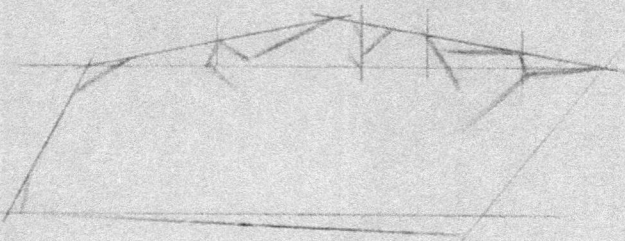

CORR. DESSIN

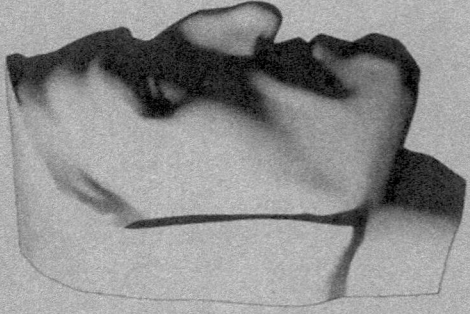

R.N.E

PL.34
K.4

DANTL

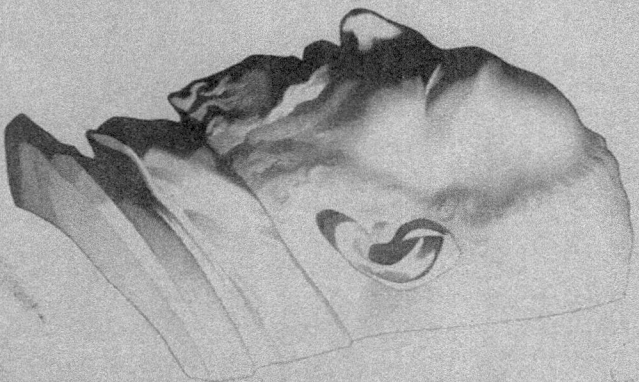

N° 35 *Report n° 1*

R N° 1

71

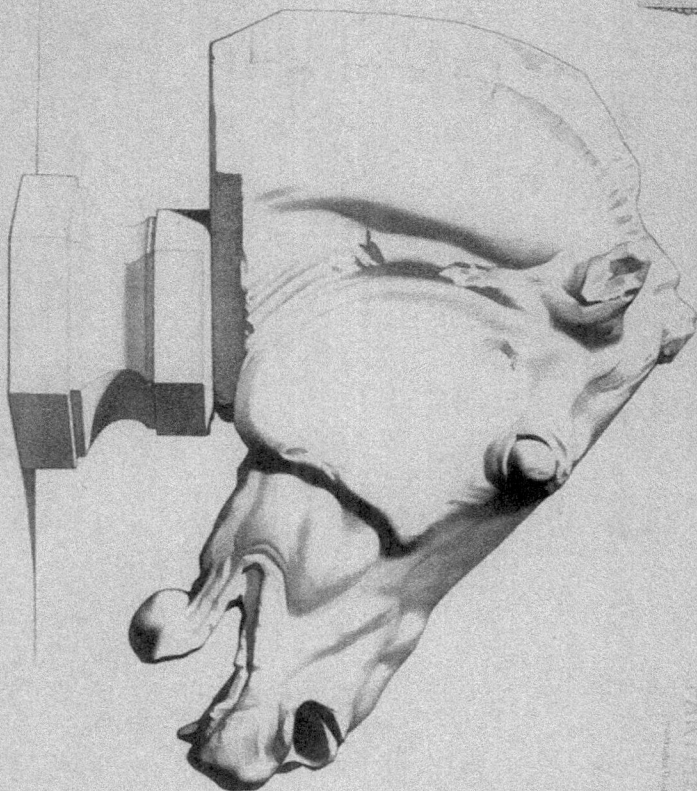

PARTHÉNON

Pierre Mêr

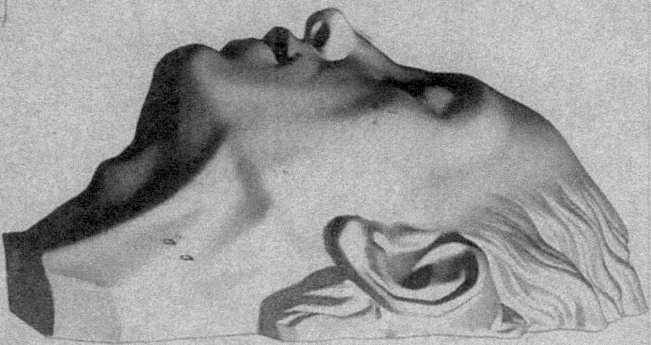

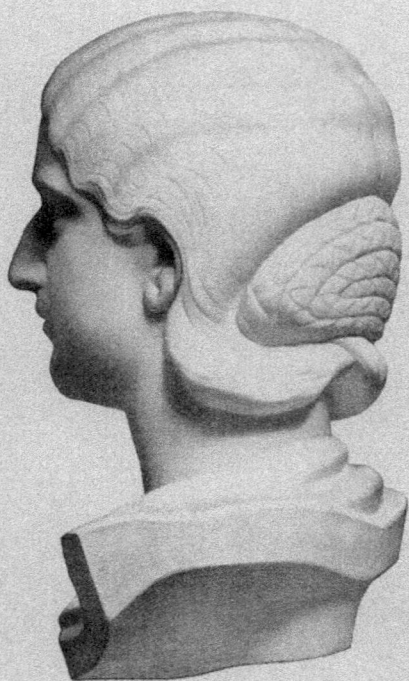

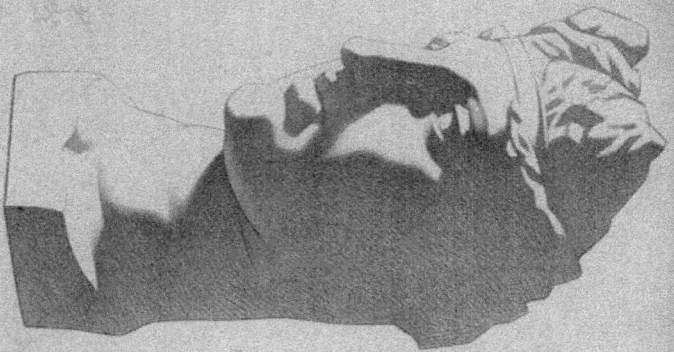

Pl. 41 Report N° 2

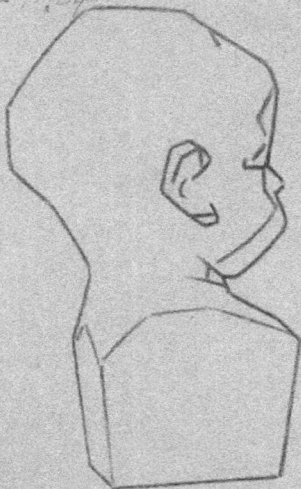
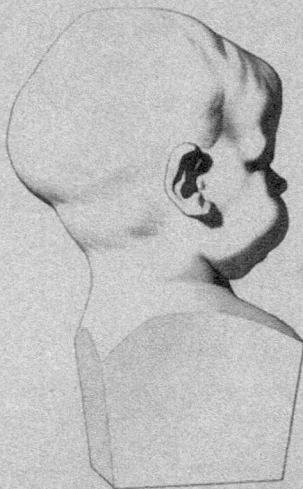

TÊTE D'ENFANT

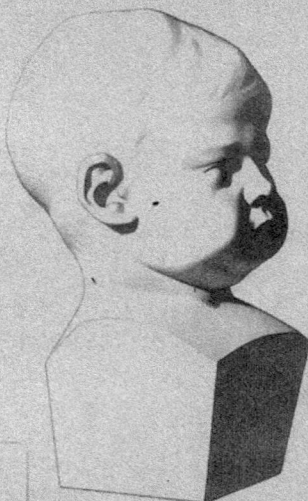

PL. 44
R. 2

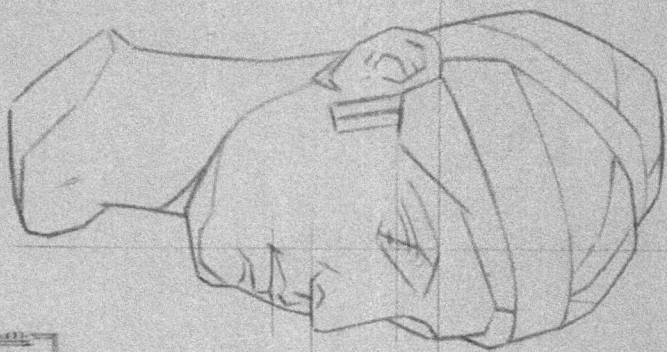

COURS DE DESSIN

FAVSTINE

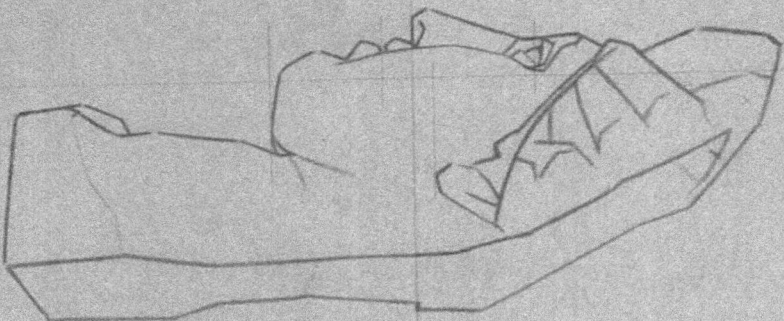

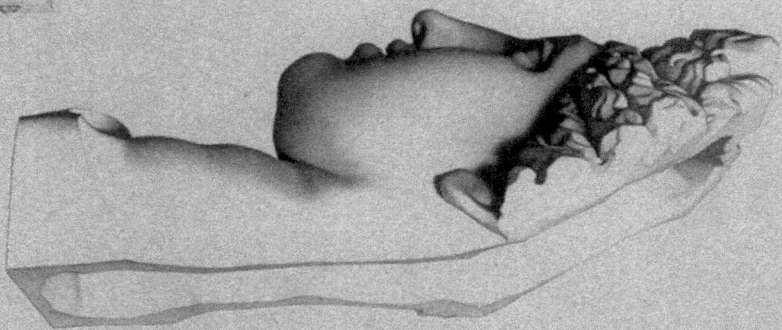

ARIANE DV CAPITOLE

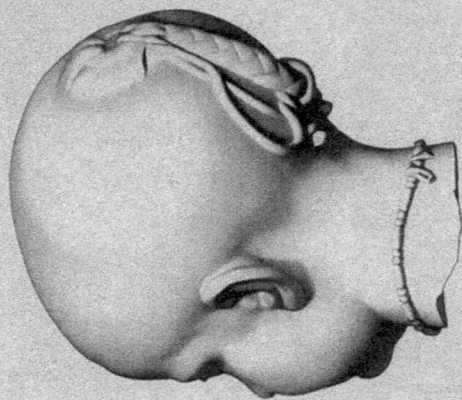

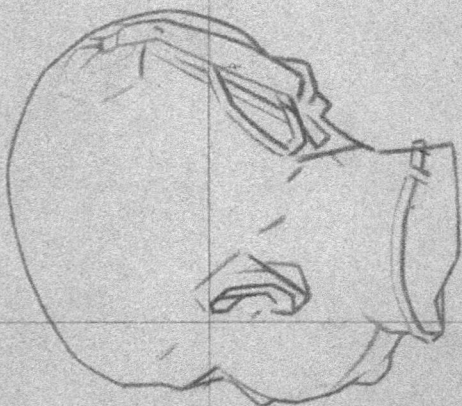

JEUNE GARÇON

— Antique —

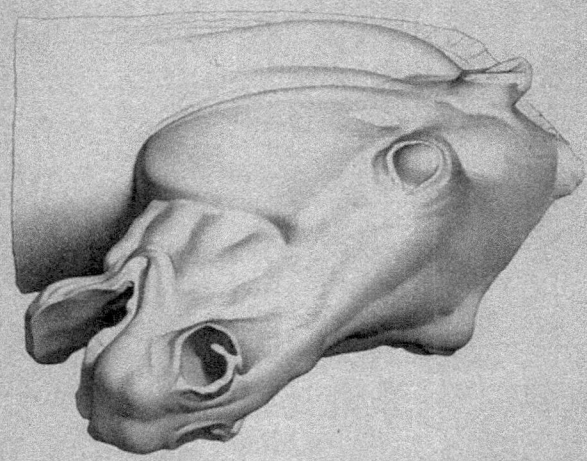

Pierre Mür

91 · 46

PHOCION

WA

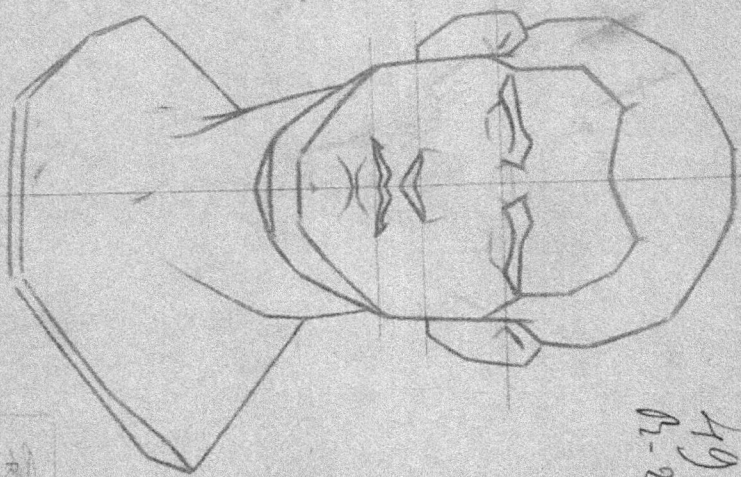

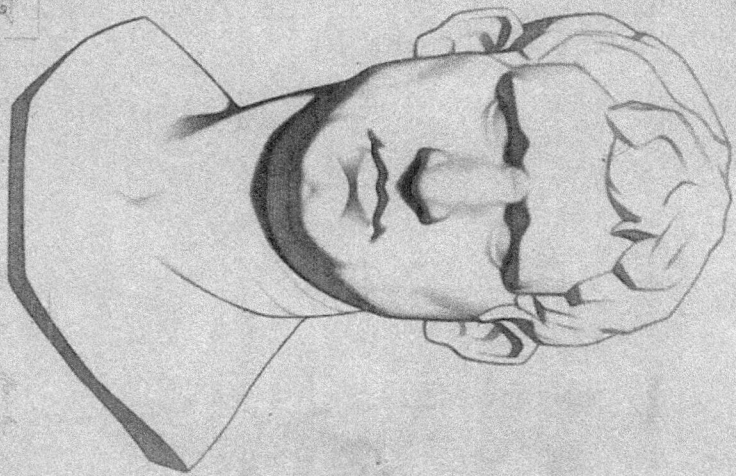

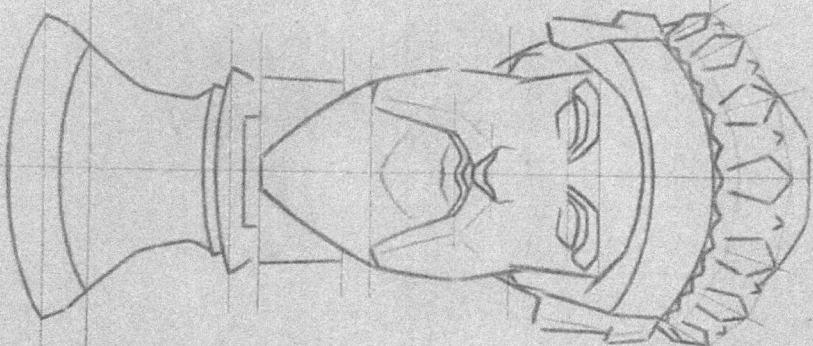

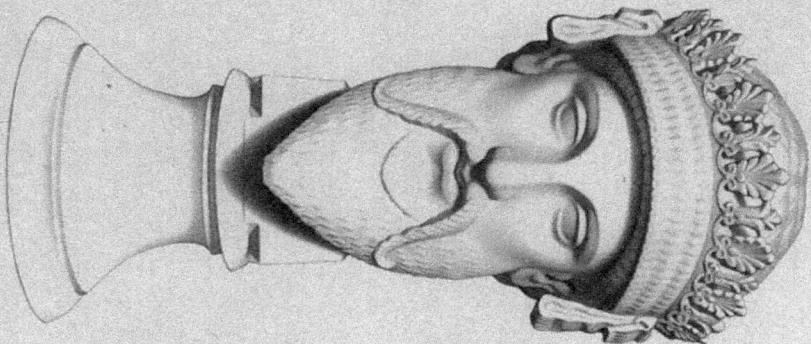

JVPITER TROPHONIVS

LVCIVS JVNIVS BRVTVS

JEVNE FEMME

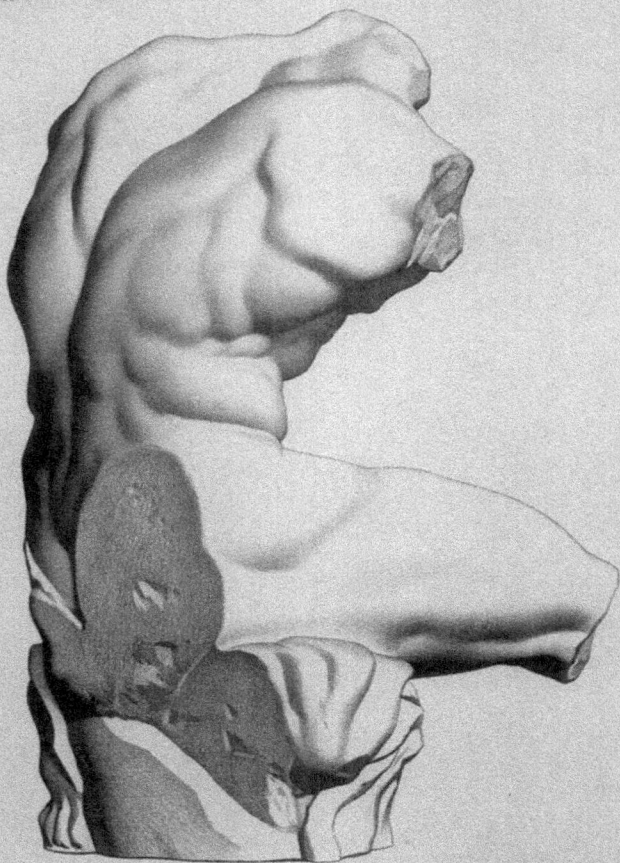

LE TORSE DV BELVEDERE

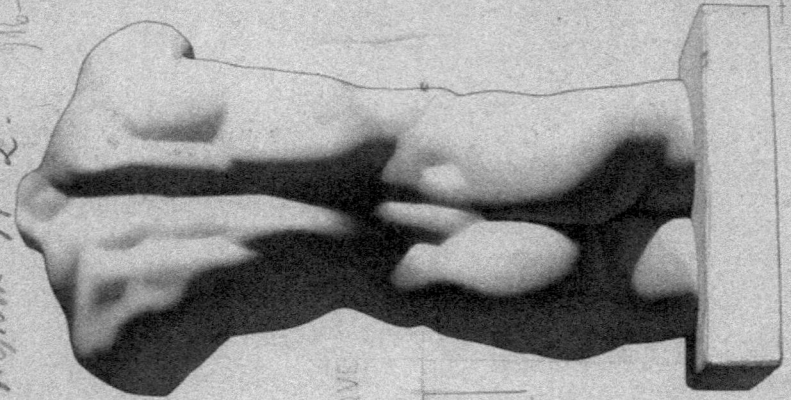

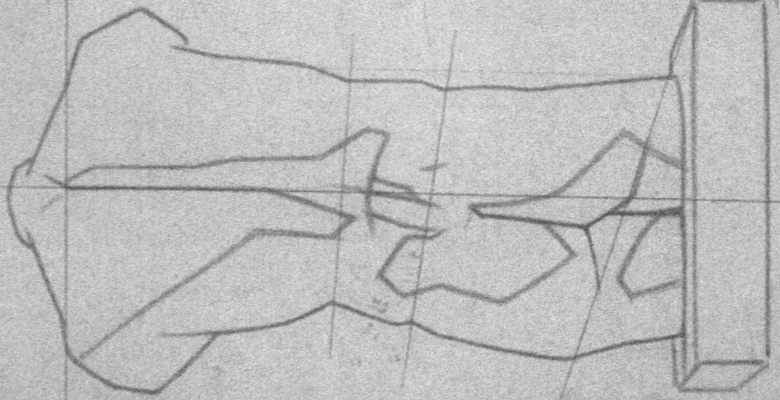

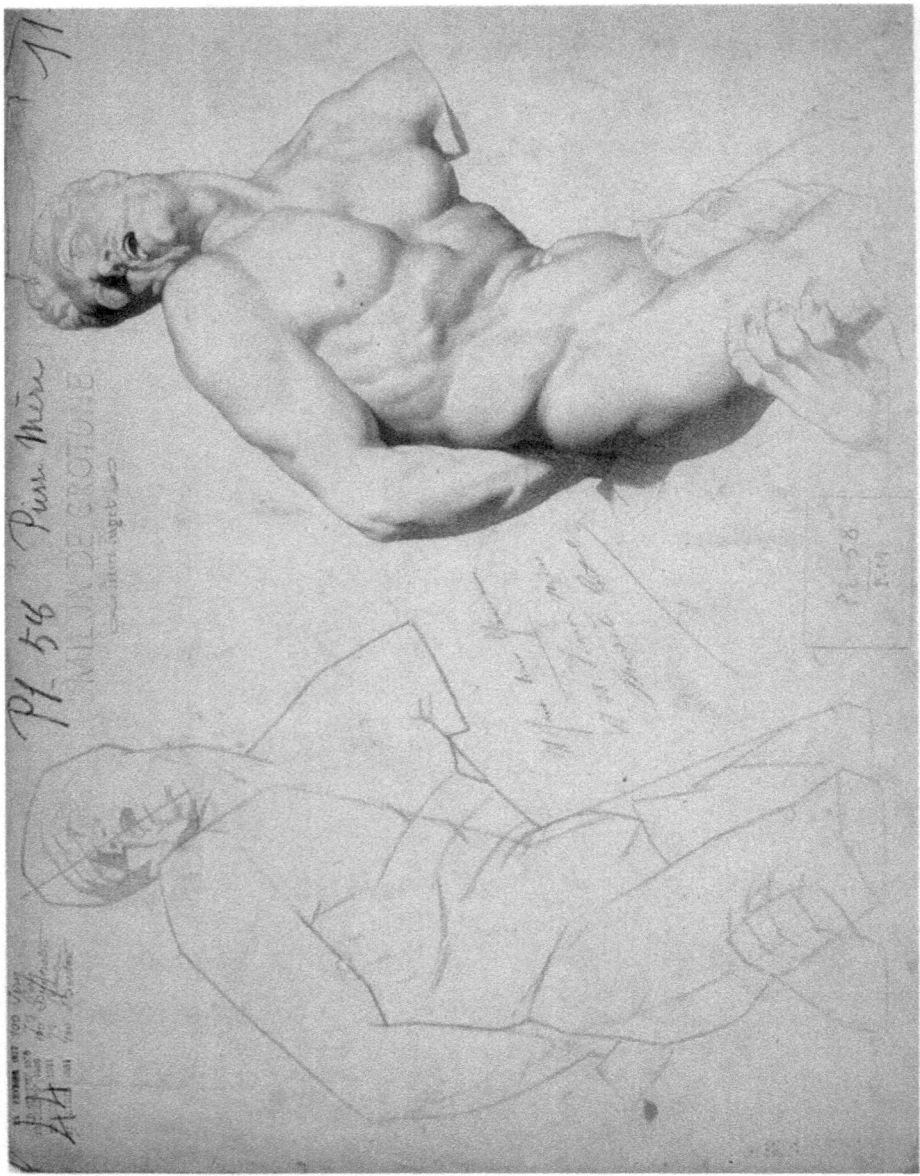

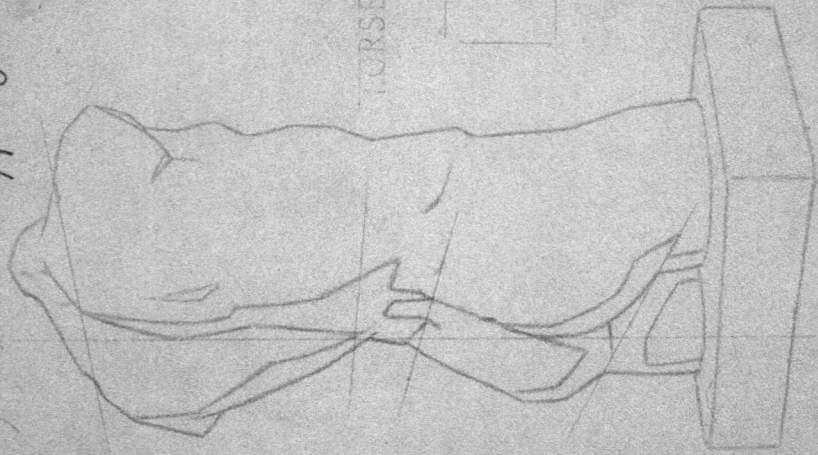

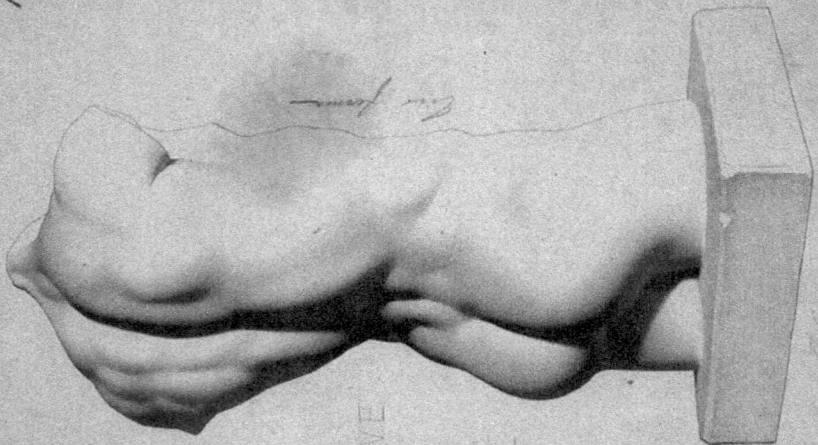

TORSE ANTIQUE

Pl. 60 / FM

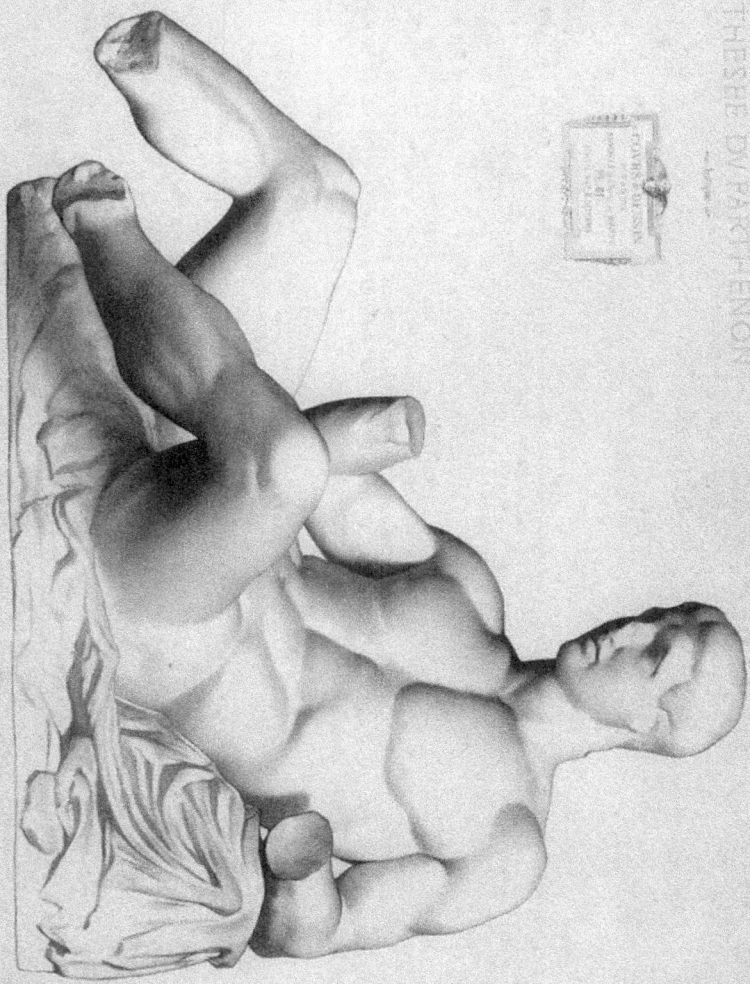
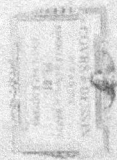

THÉSÉE DV PARTHÉNON

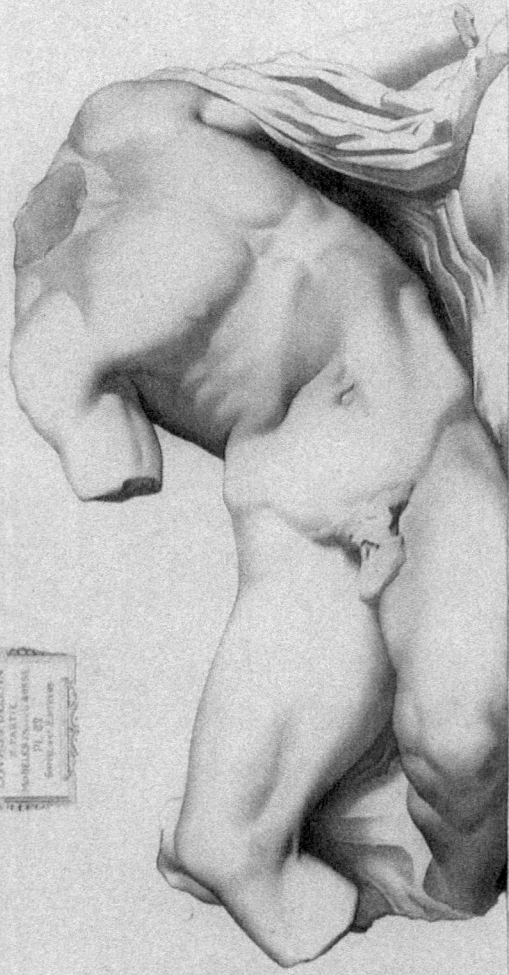

L'ILISSVS DV PARTHÉNON

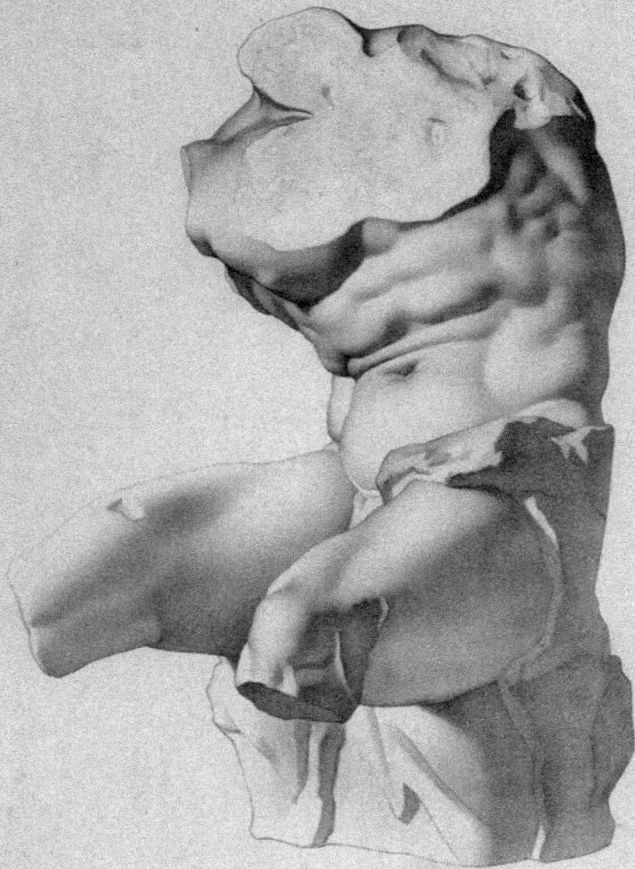

PARTHENON
Fragment de la frise

PARTHENON
— Fragments de frise .

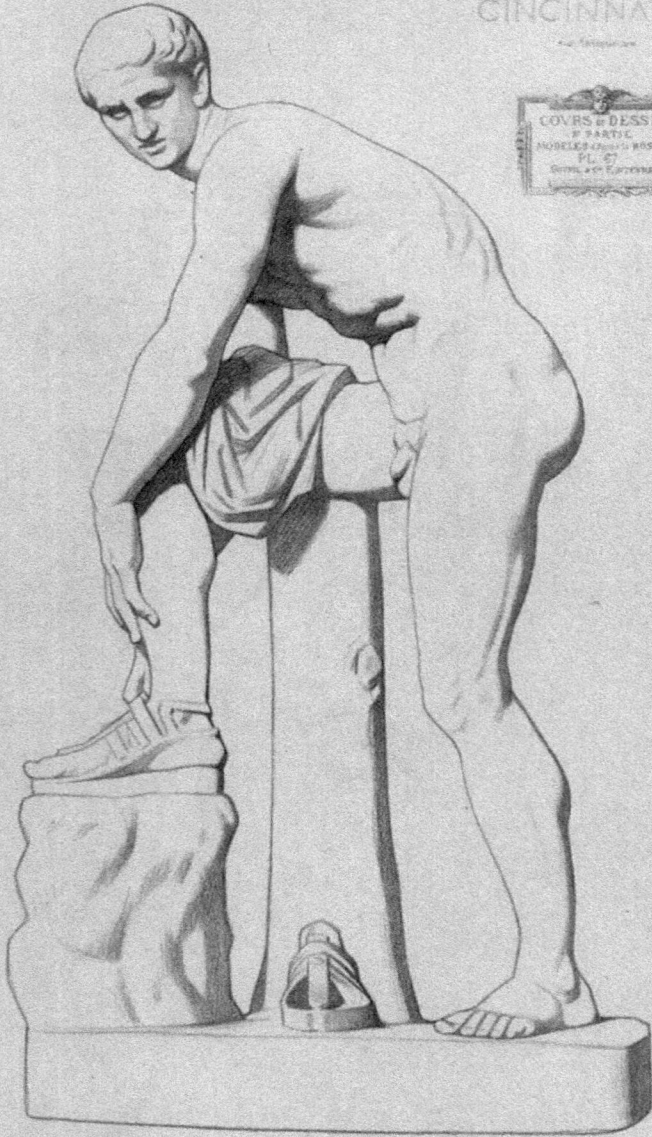

COVRS DE DESSIN
IIe PARTIE
MODELES d'après la BOSSE
PL. 47

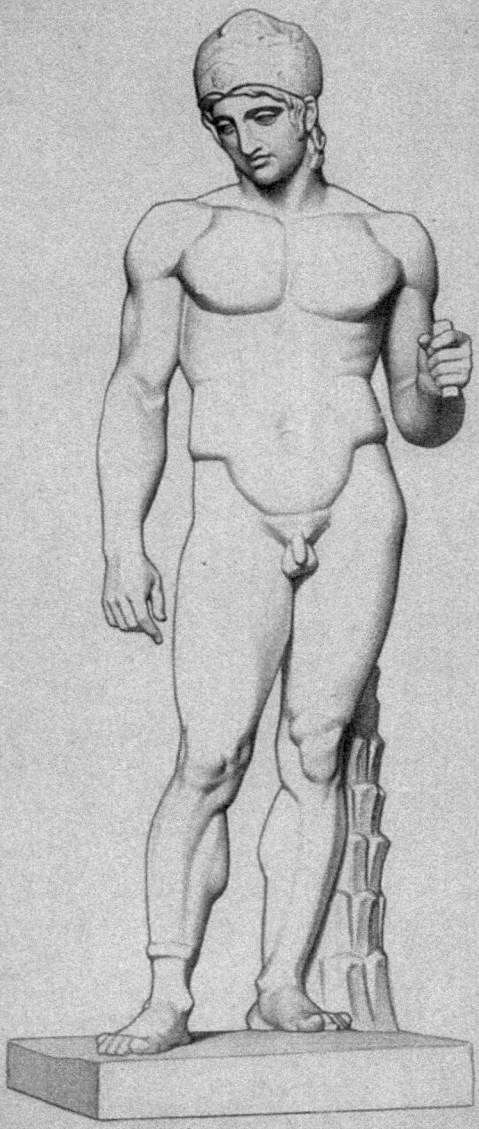

Pl. 68 Pian Atin 11.

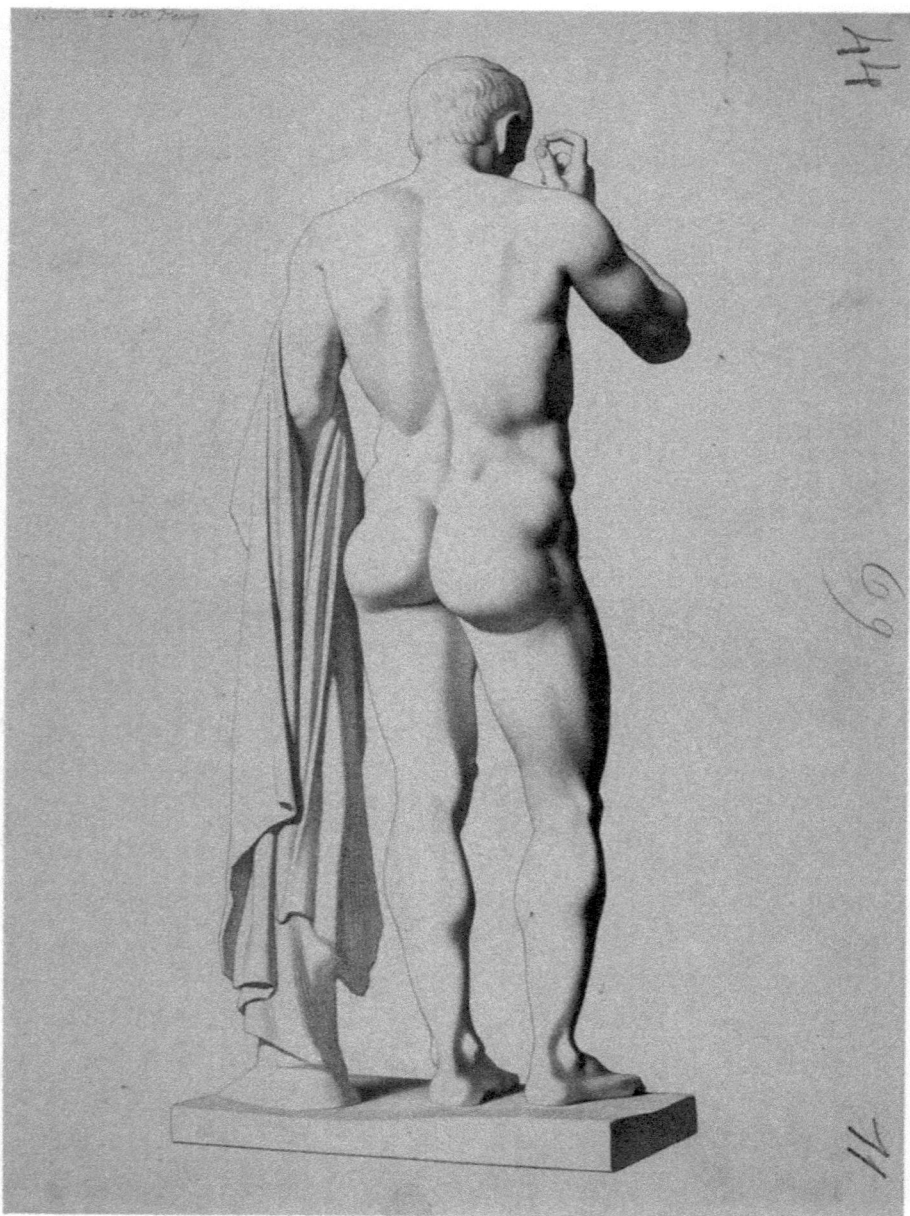

SAINTE MARTHE
Gothique

PL·70
R·I

Plate II, 1

Plate II, 2

Plate II, 3

Plate II, 4

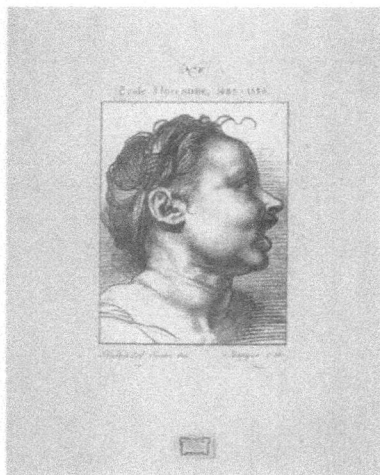

Plate II, 5

Plate II, 6

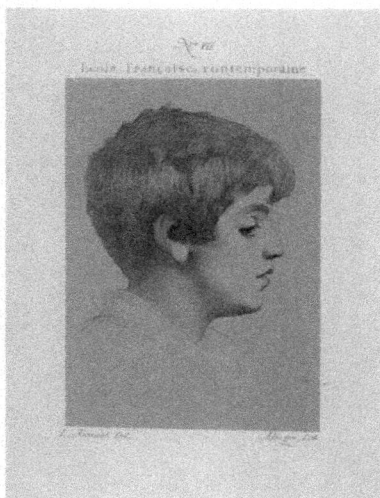

Plate II, 7

Plate II, 8

Plate II, 9

Plate II, 10

Plate II, 11

Plate II, 12

Plate II, 13

Plate II, 14

Plate II, 15

Plate II, 16

عسس
خلف
الله

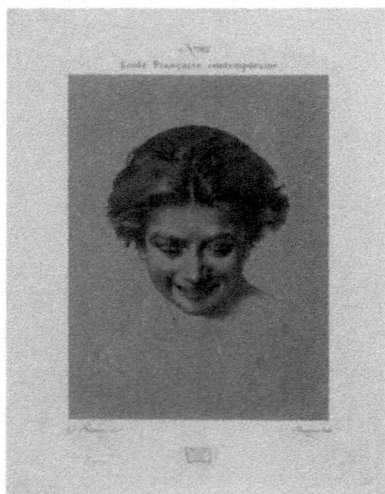

Plate II, 17

Plate II, 18

Plate II, 19

Plate II, 20

Plate II, 21

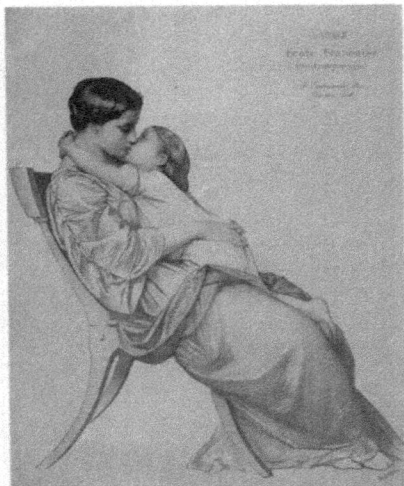

Plate II, 22

Plate II, 23

Plate II, 24

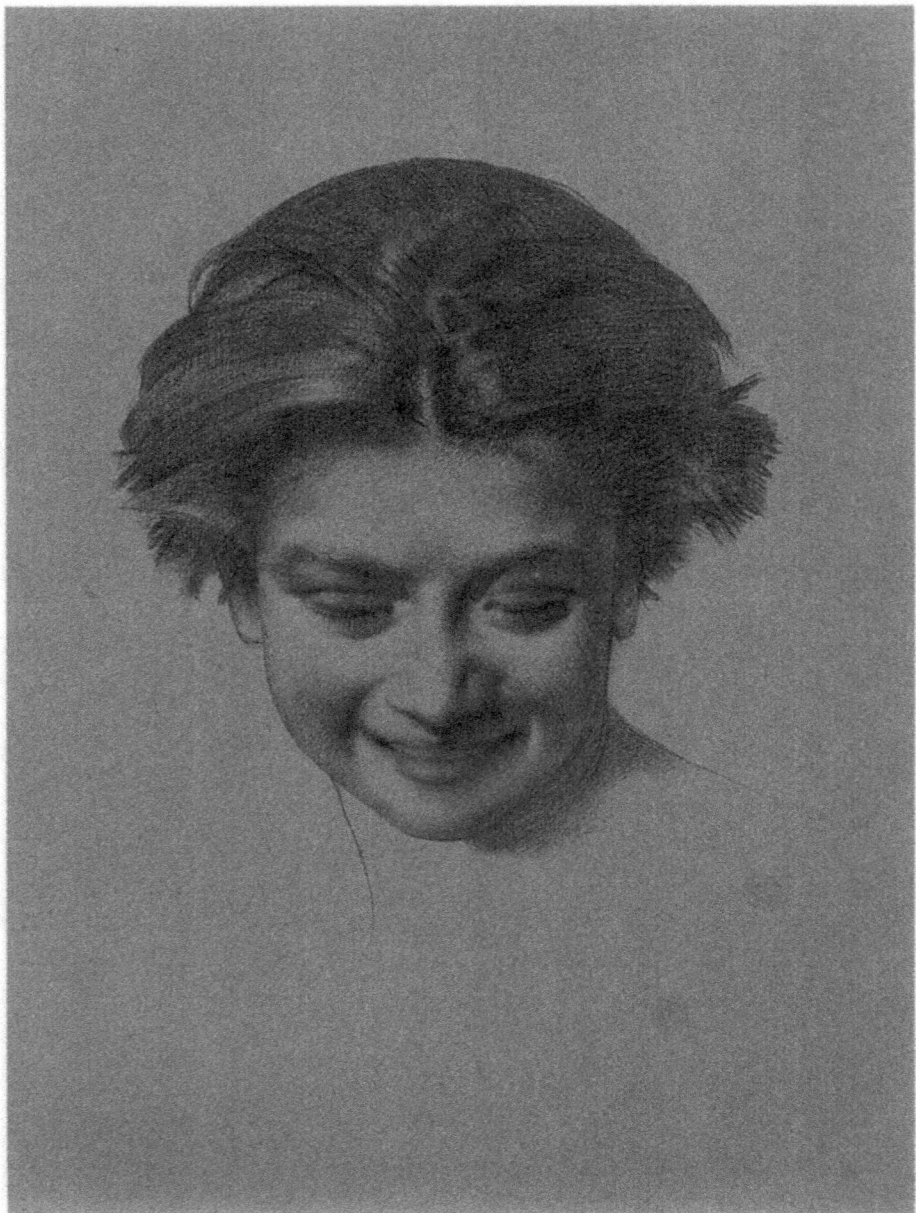

N° XVII

École Française
contemporaine

A. Vinlimache. Pini
Marjise. Lith.

Plate II, 25

Plate II, 26

Plate II, 27

Plate II, 28

Plate II, 29

Plate II, 30

Plate II, 31

Plate II, 32

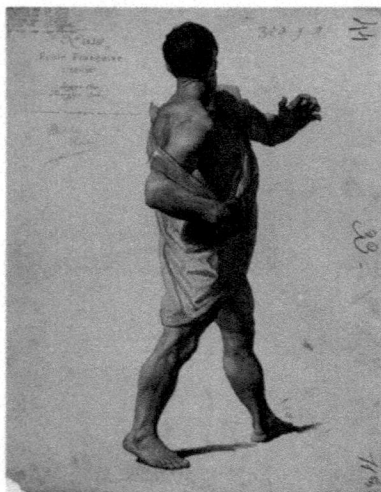

Plate II, 33

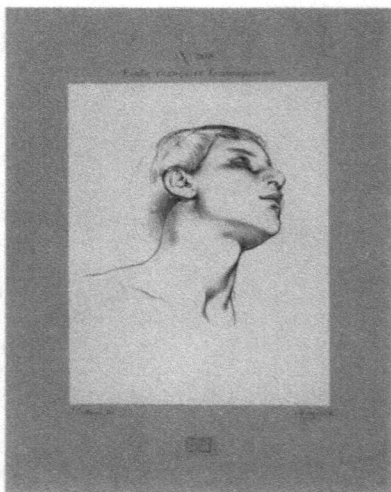

Plate II, 34

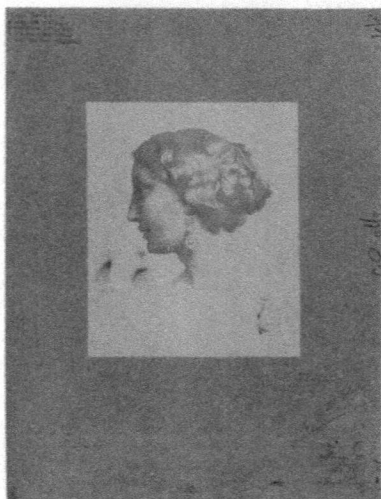

Plate II, 35

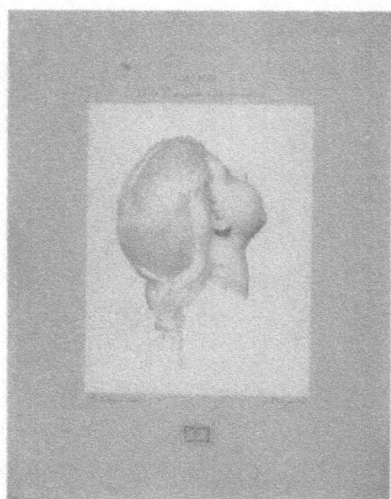

Plate II, 36

Plate II, 37

Plate II, 38

Plate II, 39

Plate II, 40

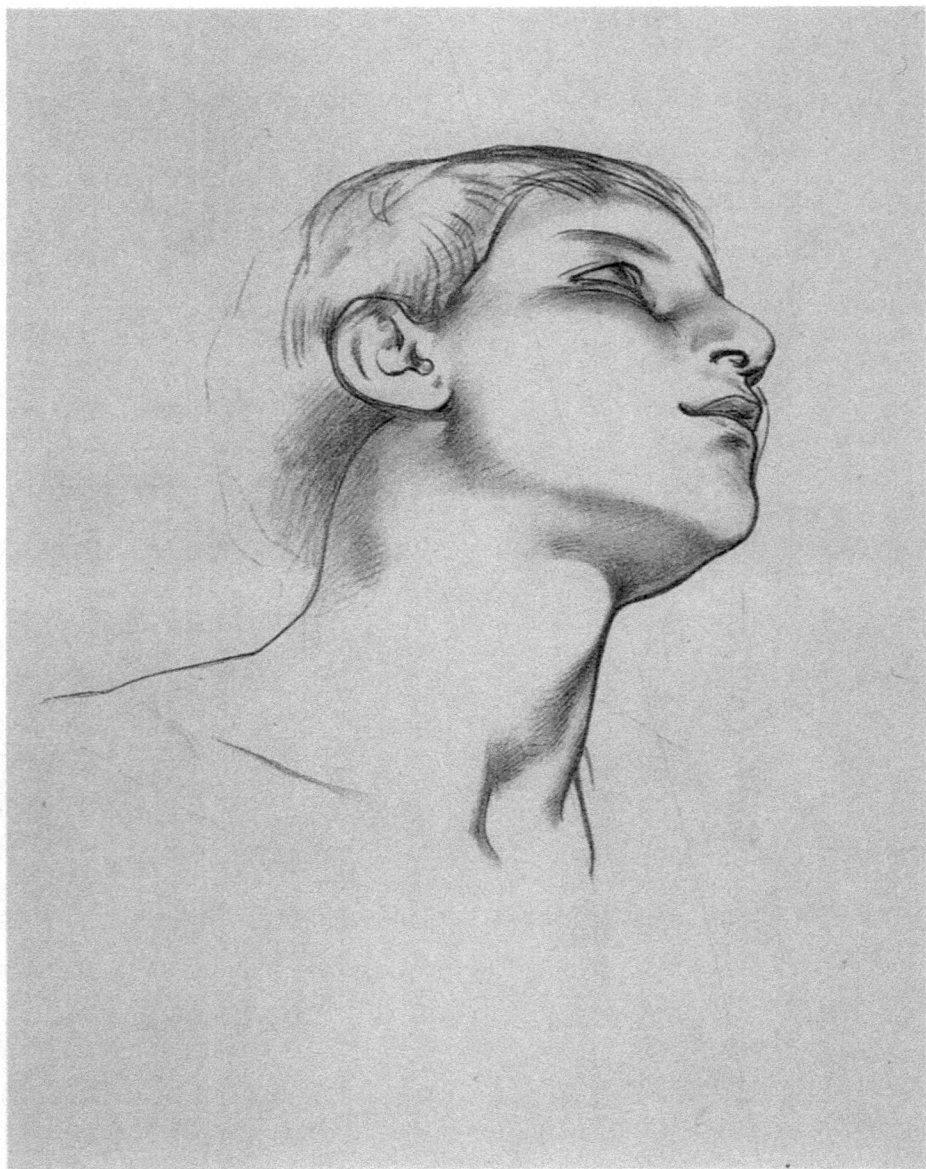

Plate II, 41

Plate II, 42

Plate II, 43

Plate II, 44

Plate II, 45

Plate II, 46

Plate II, 47

Plate II, 48

Plate II, 49

Plate II, 50

Plate II, 51

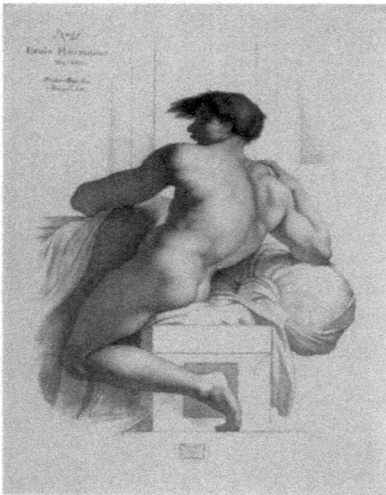

Plate II, 52

Plate II, 53

Plate II, 54

Plate II, 55

Plate II, 56

N.º LIV

École française contemporaine.

T. Schnetzen Tion
Bargue cas

Plate II, 57

Plate II, 58

Plate II, 59

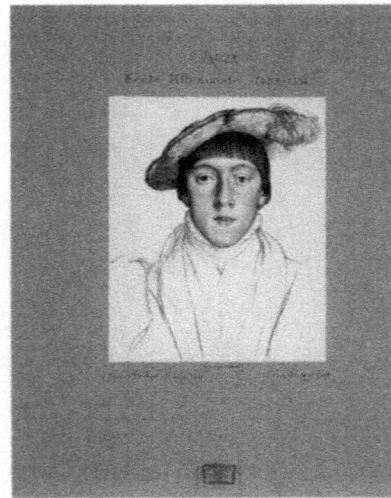

Plate II, 60

Plate II, 61

Plate II, 62

Plate II, 63

Plate II, 64

Plate II, 65

Plate II, 66

Plate II, 67

NOTES ON THE PLATES

Although all the lithographs in part II are reproduced, not all are recommended for copying. Those thought to be the best models for beginning students are reproduced as full-page illustrations and are accompanied by technical notes. The others are reproduced as quarter-page illustrations.

Plate II, 1. Michelangelo (1475–1564), *Angel Blowing a Trumpet.*
(Ange sonnant de la trompette.) Sistine Chapel, Vatican City

This drawing is an "interpretation" of a famous figure in the grand fresco *The Last Judgment* (1536-1542) in the Sistine Chapel in the Vatican.

Plate II, 2. Hippolyte Flandrin (1809–1864), *Study of a Woman.*
(Étude de femme.) Whereabouts unknown

Flandrin, a student of Ingres, was most famous for his decorations of churches and palaces. This is a preparatory drawing for the decorations done in 1841 for the duc de Luynes at his chateau in Dampierre.¹ See also plates II, 15 and II, 25.

Plate II, 3. Hippolyte Flandrin, *Italian Shepherd,* study.
(Pâtre italien [tête d'étude].*)* Whereabouts unknown

Plate II, 4. Jean-Léon Gérôme (1824–1904), *Head of a Fellah,* three-quarter view.
(Tête de fellah, vue de trois quarts.) Private collection

See the comments to plate II, 14.

Plate II, 5. Andrea del Sarto (1486–1530), *Head of a Child.*
(Tête d'enfant.) Louvre Museum, Paris

This is a drawing for a figure in the painting *Caritas*, painted in Paris in 1518. The painting is also in the Louvre Museum in Paris. See also comments to plate II, 31.

Plate II, 6. Agnolo Gaddi (1345–1396), *Portrait of a Man.*
(Portrait d'homme.) British Museum, London

The drawing has the attribution to Agnolo Gaddi inscribed on the verso. It was attributed to Masaccio by Johann David Passavant (1833) and to Domenico Ghirlandaio by Bernard Berenson (1938), an attribution retained to this day.

Plate II, 7. Léon Bonnat (1833–1922), *Young Roman,* study.
(Jeune Romain [tête d'étude].*)* Bonnat Museum, Bayonne

Bonnat was a good friend of Gérôme and accompanied him on excursions (on safari) in Egypt and Palestine on several occasions. A portrait painter noted for the illusionistic qualities of his realism, Bonnat was also a famous collector of master drawings; his collection is now in the Bonnat Museum in Bayonne.

Vigorous cross-hatching establishes the hair, showing both its growth pattern and its general planes. The roundness of the globe of the eye is described by careful construction of its darkest parts as well as by the placing of a few accents that follow the form. The subtle structure of the children's heads taxes any artist's knowledge of anatomy because the surface does not reveal the body structure.

Fig. 23.
Hans Holbein the Younger.
*The Daughter of Jakob
Meyer. (La Fille de Jacques
Meyer.)* 1525.
Black and colored
chalks. Light green wash
background on paper.
39 x 37.2 cm.
(15.5 x 14.75 in.)
Öffentliche
Kunstsammlung Basel,
Kupferstichkabinett.
Compare plate II, 10.

Plate II, 8. Hans Holbein the Younger (1497–1543), *Gentleman from the Court of Henry VIII.*
(Gentilhomme de la cour de Henri VIII.) Collection of Her Majesty the Queen, Royal Library, Windsor Castle

Hans Holbein the Younger was born in Augsburg, where he was trained by his father, Hans Holbein the Elder, a noted artist. He worked first in Prague and Basel. After traveling in Italy and France, he went to London, where he became court painter to Henry VIII. He sketched and painted many members of the court in a frank and objective style. His drawings are the most frequently reproduced in part II.

Plate II, 9. Hans Holbein the Younger, *Sir Nicholas Carew.*
(Sir Nicolas Carew.) Öffentliche Kunstsammlung Basel, Kupferstichkabinett

Sir Nicolas was an *écuyer*, or squire, in charge of the stables of Henry VIII.

Plate II, 10. Hans Holbein the Younger, *The Daughter of Jacques Meyer.*
(La fille de Jacques Meyer.) 1525. Öffentliche Kunstsammlung Basel, Kupferstichkabinett

This drawing of Anna Meyer is a preparatory drawing for a portrait in the Gemäldegalerie Alte Meister, Staatliche Kunstsammlungen, Dresden.

If you look ahead to the portraits by Paul Dubois (plate II, 18) and Adolphe-William Bouguereau (plate II, 23), you will see that Holbein has more carefully delineated each element—including facial features and costume—than either artist. Yet both Dubois and Bouguereau have outlined the contours of the face with great subtlety, noting the sitter's anatomy: the forehead, the brow, the cheekbone, the nose, the fullness of the cheek and of the muscles around the mouth, and the protuberance of the chin. Study each drawing. Try to understand the reason for each bump or depression of the face; refer to an anatomy book for guidance. The light is frontal but diffused. Lighter areas are modeled by veiling. Compare this drawing with the photograph of the original drawing, done in black and colored chalks against a green background (see fig. 23).

Plate II, 11. Raphael (1483–1520), *Kneeling Woman.*
(Figure de femme agenouillée.) Pinacoteca Vaticana, Vatican City

The drawing is after a figure in Raphael's oil painting, *The Transfiguration* (painted between 1517 and 1520), in the Pinacoteca Vaticana, Vatican City.

Plate II, 12. Filippino Lippi (1457–1504), *Portrait.*
(Portrait de Filippino Lippi.) Ufizzi Gallery, Florence

This is an "interpretation," that is, a drawing after a finished work, in this case a self-portrait in fresco (probably a fragment of a wall decoration). Fresco technique requires broad handling. Whereas Bonnat (see plate II, 7) had used hatching for shading, here the artist uses a sfumato—a gentle modeling by means of an overlapping, blended succession of values—in a dramatic chiaroscuro. The light on the right side reveals the fleshy roundness of the artist's parted lips. The direction of the illumination—frontal lighting slightly off to one side—causes a raking shadow and sets the mood of the portrait. A slightly agitated youth emerges from the shadowed uncertainty of adolescence.

Plate II, 13. Charles Gleyre (1808–1874), *Omphale*, study.
(Omphale [tête d'étude].*)* Whereabouts unknown

Gleyre was one of Gérôme's teachers. This is a study "from nature" for the painting *Hercules at the Feet of Omphale (Hercule aux pieds d'Omphale)*, now in the Musée Cantonal des Beaux-Arts, Lausanne. William Hauptman thinks the drawing was done by Gleyre expressly for the *Drawing Course;* he also notes that Diego Rivera (1886–1957) copied this lithograph while a student in Madrid.[17]

Gleyre's interpretation of the Greek portrait style is modified by his working from life. The frontal lighting pushes most of the darker tints to the edges, emphasizing the outline. The expression is tender yet ambiguous, as is the modeling, which describes Omphale's features in a thin veil of tone.

Plate II, 14. Jean-Léon Gérôme (1824–1904), *Head of a Fellah*, profile. (*Tête de fellah, vue de profil.*) Private collection

A fellah is an Egyptian peasant. This sketch was made while traveling on safari in Egypt during the winter of 1856–57: the young man was probably a retainer. Gérôme also engraved the portrait.

Gérôme uses a device that successfully focuses our interest on the face: he finishes the features, while handling the clothing in a sketchier style. His cross-hatching is very vigorous. Gérôme was obviously attracted to the pronounced, punctuated features of the young Arab. Compare the handling of this head with Gleyre's treatment of a young girl's head in plate II, 36.

Plate II, 15. Hippolyte Flandrin, *Study of a Woman*. (*Étude de femme.*) Whereabouts unknown

This is a preparatory drawing for the decorations done in 1841 for the duc de Luynes at his chateau in Dampierre. See also comments to plates II, 2 and II, 25.

Flandrin has reserved the most pronounced modeling for the contours, an effect produced more naturally by Gleyre (see plate II, 13). These are not actual shadows but rather a darkening of light areas with cross-hatchings, the effect of frontal lighting. Like Gérôme, Flandrin has described the drapery sketchily, although not enough to disturb the classical, intellectual imitation of Greek vase painting behind the pose of the woman and her chair. Compare the idealized portrait of the woman with the cast drawing of a Roman empress (plate I, 43), the depiction of her body to Raphael's clothed figure (plates II, 11 and II, 43), and the modeling of the outstretched hand to that of the cast drawing of a woman pressing her breast with her hand (plate I, 15).

Plate II, 16. Raphael, *Self-Portrait*. (*Portrait de Raphael.*) Uffizi Gallery, Florence

This drawing is an "interpretation" after an early painting by Raphael also in the Uffizi.

Plate II, 17. Jean-Jacques Henner (1829–1905), *Laughing Boy*, study. (*Le Rieur* [tête d'étude].) Whereabouts unknown

Henner was famous for nudes painted in a developed chiaroscuro. His house in Paris is now the Musée national Jean-Jacques Henner.

Strongly animated heads are in the tradition both of Hellenistic sculpture and of the sculpted *têtes d'expression*, or expressive heads (that is, heads showing specific emotions) produced by students at the École des Beaux-Arts in Paris (see also *concours* in glossary). Henner combines all three methods of shading—stumping, hatching, and veiling—in this lively head. Seen from above, the hair becomes the dominant feature. The view was chosen to add movement to the figure and to support the expression on the boy's face. The hair is decorative yet still true to the values one might see in nature. The part breaks the hair up into sections that follow the growth pattern.

Plate II, 18. Paul Dubois (1829–1905), *Roman Woman*. (*femme romaine.*) Whereabouts unknown

Dubois was an excellent sculptor whose work was influenced by Florentine quattrocento sculpture. He was a student at the École des Beaux-Arts in Paris, where even sculptors were taught to draw well.

By deliberately putting his model in profile, Dubois emphasizes the abstract and formal qualities of the picture rather than the personality of the sitter. Her features are described in halftones that contrast with the light background and further distinguish the contours. Both stumping and veiling techniques could have achieved the painterly qualities of this drawing. Whereas Gérôme suppressed most of the values of the face in his portraits of Arabs, Dubois describes every change in values—and he finishes the clothing and accessories as well.

Plate II, 19. Hans Holbein the Younger, *Sir Charles Elliot*.
(Le chevalier Charles Elliot.) Collection of Her Majesty the Queen, Royal Library, Windsor Castle

Plate II, 20. Hans Holbein the Younger, *Gentleman from the Court of Henry VIII*.
(Gentilhomme de la cour de Henri VIII.) Collection of Her Majesty the Queen, Royal Library, Windsor Castle

Plate II, 21. Michelangelo, *Study of a Man*.
(Étude d'homme.) Sistine Chapel, Vatican City

This is another "interpretation" after a figure in the *Last Judgment* fresco (1536-1542) in the Sistine Chapel. It is a lesson in foreshortening.

Plate II, 22. Auguste Toulmouche (1829–1890), *Young Woman Kissing Her Child*.
(Jeune femme embrassant son enfant.) Whereabouts unknown

Like Gérôme, Toulmouche was a student of Gleyre. He and Gérôme also belonged to the Néo-Grecs, a group of young painters of the mid-nineteenth century who painted genre scenes set in antiquity. Toulmouche soon switched to contemporary genre scenes, depicting middle-class women and their children. This pair was also used in a lost painting entitled *The Maternal Kiss (Le Baiser maternel)*, which was shown at the Salon of 1857.

The lighting is frontal. Both interlocked figures are seen in profile. Toulmouche uses subtle changes in perspective to create rhythms that move forward as well as up and down.

Plate II, 23. Adolphe-William Bouguereau (1825–1905), *A Roman Woman*, study.
(Tête de femme romaine [étude].) Whereabouts unknown

Bouguereau was almost an exact contemporary of Gérôme. Along with Ernest Meissonier (1815–1891), they were the most famous representatives of French Academic Realism of the second half of the nineteenth century.

Bouguereau's use of loose hatch lines is closer to Gérôme's methods than to the hatching of Dubois. He probably drew this in pencil—the shadows of the hair and figure are rather light—reserving the darks for the accents in the eye, nose, mouth, and ear.

Plate II, 24. *Archer from Aegina*.
(Sagittaire Éginète.) Staatliche Antikensammlungen und Glyptothek, Munich

This is a figure (480 B.C.) from the east pediment of the Doric temple of Aphia on the island of Aegina. The lion-head cap identifies him as Hercules. In the early nineteenth century the twelve figures of the pediment were restored by the great Danish Neoclassical sculptor Bertl Thorvaldsen (1770-1884). The draftsman has chosen a view of the statue where the restorations are least evident, which includes the right forearm, the left hand, the left thigh, part of the right foot, and parts of the hem of the skirt (see also plate II, 40).

Plate II, 25. Hippolyte Flandrin, *Study of a Woman*.
(Étude de femme.) Whereabouts unknown

This is yet another drawing for the decoration of the chateau of the duc de Luynes in Dampierre; see comments to plates II, 2 and II, 15.

This drawing shows a woman drying her hair after a bath. The most remarkable feature is the continuous, unbroken line describing the left contour of the figure. Even though the character of the figure is round and voluptuous, the outline is stabilized by straight passages. Moreover, its linear, decorative quality vies with its ability to express volume. As with the other nude studies prepared for the Dampierre decorations, there is very little interior modeling. Dark accents are prominent only in the features of the face. With a little practice the student will be able to see how the drawing differs from nature, how Flandrin abstracts and flattens the figure to achieve his conception of the ideal, and which aspects of the figure he chooses to stress—such as the facial expression—and which he chooses to suppress. The simplicity of the drawing is deceptive. Flandrin's style is practiced yet truthful in its larger concepts: the muscles and morphological forms fit together, and a minimum of tones reveals these forms. The lighting is similar to the drawing of the cast of the *Achilles* (see plate I, 68).

Plate II, 26. Hans Holbein the Younger, *Citizen of Basel*.
(Bourgeoise de Bâle.) Öffentliche Kunstsammlung Basel, Kupferstichkabinett

Plate II, 27. Hans Holbein the Younger, *Anna Grisacria*.
(Anna Grisacria [Cresacre].) Collection of Her Majesty the Queen, Royal Library, Windsor Castle

Plate II, 28. Hans Holbein the Younger, *John Poines*.
(John Poines.) Collection of Her Majesty the Queen, Royal Library, Windsor Castle

Plate II, 29. Hans Holbein the Younger, *Thomas, Count of Surrey*.
(Thomas, comte de Surrey.) Collection of Her Majesty the Queen, Royal Library, Windsor Castle

The sitter is now identified as Henry Howard, earl of Surrey.

Plate II, 30. Hans Holbein the Younger, *Anne Boleyn*.
(Anne Boleyn.) Collection of Her Majesty the Queen, Royal Library, Windsor Castle

Plate II, 31. Andrea del Sarto (1486–1530), *Self-Portrait*.
(Portrait d'Andrea del Sarto.) Whereabouts unknown

This is an "interpretation," a drawing after a finished painting, *Charity*, (1486) in the Uffizi Gallery, Florence. Andrea del Sarto was one of the great masters of the Italian Renaissance, whose major works are in the Pitti Palace in Florence.

Andrea's treatment is more realistic than that of Gleyre and Flandrin. He attends to all the major forms of the face, putting them in tonally by means of stumping. The eyes are circumscribed by halftones that give clarity to the skeletal sockets. Compare this with plate II, 12.

Plate II, 32. Raphael, *Dante*.
(Portrait du Dante.) Stanze di Raffaello, Vatican City

This is a drawing after the figure of Dante in the fresco *Parnassus* located in the Stanza della Segnatura (1508–11) in the Vatican. Raphael developed his likeness from older, traditional portraits of Dante.

Plate II, 33. Jean-Auguste-Dominique Ingres (1780–1867), *A Lictor*. *(Licteur.)* Ingres Museum, Montauban

This is an "interpretation" after a famous oil sketch in the Ingres Museum in Montauban. The oil sketch was a study for a large painting entitled *The Martyrdom of Saint Symphorian (Le Martyre de saint Symphorien)* (1834) in the Cathedral of Saint Lazare, Autun.

Plate II, 34. Jules Lefebvre (1836–1912), *Head of a Child*. *(Tête d'enfant.)* Whereabouts unknown

Lefebvre was a successful academic painter, famous for his nudes, and a longtime teacher at the Académie Julian in Paris. Although he received many decorations, honors, and state commissions, he is hardly remembered today, although several of his works are still admired and reproduced.

This is a preparatory drawing for his painting *Cornelia, Mother of the Gracchi (Cornélie, mère des Gracques)*, whose present location is unknown. This is a masterful study of a foreshortened head, seen from below, as well as an example of "stopped modeling." The halftones are produced both by stumping and hatching. Thick and thin lines form the contours, which are darkest on the shaded side of the head. The neck is a cylinder that meets the shadowy underside of the chin. The mastoid muscle *(sternocleidomastoideus)* is fully described under the ear, as is its attachment to the clavicle below the lightly hatched Adam's apple.

Plate II, 35. Émile Lévy (1826–1890), *Head of a Young Italian Girl*. *(Tête de jeune fille italienne.)* Whereabouts unknown

Émile Lévy was a student of François-Édouard Picot (1786–1868) and Alexandre Denis Abel Pujol (1787–1861). Winner of a Prix de Rome in history painting in 1854, he had a long career as a history and genre painter. Since his death he has slipped into obscurity. Although a contemporary of Gérôme and Bouguereau, he adhered to the conventions of Neoclassicism and avoided the more strident traits of Realism.

To copy this, use red or sanguine conté or chalk. It might be helpful to look again at the classical profiles in plates I, 33 and I, 40. The design of the hair is especially fine in its controlled ornamentation. The contour is stressed, as in many of the drawings. The lips are parted but still planar. Although each feature of the profile is carefully articulated, there is less detail in the interior modeling, with its sfumato, diffused shadows, and nebulous halftones.

Plate II, 36. Charles Gleyre, *Head of a Young Italian Girl*. *(Tête de jeune fille italienne.)* Whereabouts unknown

On Gleyre, see comments to plate II, 13. William Hauptman has identified the subject as either a study for or after the figure in the painting *La Charmeuse* of 1878, in the Kunstmuseum Basel. He postulates that the drawing might have been commissioned by Goupil for the *Drawing Course.*[38]

Use red or sanguine chalk. This is another unusual and instructive view complicated by the plumpness—more fat than muscle—of the child. Axial and vertical hatching describe the top and lower planes of the simplified hair. The prominent ear is fully finished, as are the values of the face. Note that the ear does not distract from the beauty of the modeling along the contour of the neck and face. The integrity of the head is maintained because the ear is seen in proper value relationship to the whole. The dark values inside the ear are lighter than the dark values under the ear and chin. If the values in the ear were too dark, they would draw attention to the ear.

Plate II, 37. Adolphe-William Bouguereau, *A Pifferaro*. Study painted from life. *(Pifferaro. [Étude peinte d'après nature].)* Whereabouts unknown

A *pifferaro* was a music-playing Italian shepherd, usually equipped with a rustic bagpipe or a bassoon. (The duet for oboe and bassoon in the country dance movement of Beethoven "Pastoral" Symphony imitates the *pifferari*.) In the nineteenth century they were for hire as party entertainers and models for painters.

Plate II, 38. Hans Holbein the Younger, *Portrait of Sir John Godsalve.* *(Portrait de Sir John Godsalve.)* Collection of Her Majesty the Queen, Royal Library, Windsor Castle

On Holbein, see the comments to plate II, 8. This plate is not a facsimile but rather another "interpretation" of a finished work.

The features are precise; the eyes have both upper and lower lids. The sharpness of the features differs from the two Italian portraits (plates II, 12 and II, 31). The device of a fully modeled head contrasting with a strictly linear body—although extrapolated from the finished drawing by the copyist—was nonetheless employed by Holbein in other drawings.

Plate II, 39. Hans Holbein the Younger, *Erasmus of Rotterdam.* *(Érasme.)* Louvre Museum, Paris

This is a partially finished "interpretation" of Holbein's oil portrait of the great humanist scholar. The oil is also in the Louvre Museum in Paris.

Plate II, 40. *Archer from Aegina, Wearing a Helmet.* *(Sagittaire Éginète, casqué.)* Staatliche Antikensammlungen und Glyptothek, Munich

This statue (480 B.C.) is a concoction of ancient and modern parts assembled and carved by Thorwaldsen to complete the damaged figure of an archer from the west pediment of the Doric temple of Aphia on the island of Aegina. Thorwaldsen was attempting to make an archer for the left side of the triangular pediment to balance the relatively lightly restored Hercules as archer from the other side of the pediment (see plate II, 24). New are parts of the helmet and its crest, the head, both forearms, the hem of the skirt, the lower part of the left leg and foot, and part of the right leg and foot. These restorations are not identified in the drawing, although they were evident *in situ* because of the differences in color of the old and new marble. Thorwaldsen's additions were removed in the 1960s, making the remains purely antique but destroying a great nineteenth-century conception of a primitive Greek warrior.

Plate II, 41. Michelangelo, *Man Pulling a Rope.* *(Homme au chapelet.)* Sistine Chapel, Vatican City

This is yet another figure from Michelangelo's *Last Judgment* fresco in the Sistine Chapel in the Vatican, painted between 1536 and 1542.

Plate II, 42. Michelangelo, *Eve.* *(Ève.)* Sistine Chapel, Vatican City

This figure was painted between 1508 and 1512.

Plate II, 43. Raphael, *Woman Carrying Vases.* *(Femme portant des vases.)* Sistine Chapel, Vatican City

This drawing is after a famous, oft-copied figure in the fresco *Fire in the Borgo (Incendio di Borgo)*, completed in 1514–17.

Plate II, 44. Raphael, *The Violinist.* *(Le joueur de violon.)* Sciarra Collection, Rome

Now ascribed to Sebastiano del Piombo (1485–1547), it was much admired as a Raphael in the nineteenth century. As a student in Rome in the early 1840s, Gérôme painted a copy; perhaps he supplied the painting or a drawing as the model for the lithograph. He certainly suggested its inclusion.[39] The oil was not only admired by Gérôme but was also praised by both Bouguereau and Eugène-Emmanuel Amaury-Duval (1806–1885). Although most of the Sciarra collection was sold in 1898–99, *The Violinist* is still in the collection in Rome.

Plate II, 45. Hans Holbein the Younger, *Portrait of Brooke*.
(Portrait de Brooke.) Collection of Her Majesty the Queen, Royal Library, Windsor Castle

The sitter is George Brooke, ninth baron of Cobham.

Plate II, 46. Hans Holbein the Younger, *Portrait of a Lady*.
(Portrait de femme.) Collection of Her Majesty the Queen, Royal Library, Windsor Castle

Plate II, 47. Hans Holbein the Younger, *Portrait of Lady Elliot*.
(Portrait de lady Elliot.) Collection of Her Majesty the Queen, Royal Library, Windsor Castle

The sitter is Margaret, Lady Elliot. Her name is misspelled on the drawing.

Plate II, 48. Hans Holbein the Younger, *Portrait of William, marquess of Northampton*.
(Portrait de William, marquess de Northampton.) Collection of Her Majesty the Queen, Royal Library, Windsor Castle

The sitter is William Parr, first marquess of Northampton.

Plate II, 49. Jules Breton (1827–1905), *The Servant*.
(La servante.) Whereabouts unknown

This is a "facsimile of a drawing after nature." A contemporary of Gérôme, Pierre Puvis de Chavannes (1824–1898) and Bouguereau, Breton was a famous and prolific painter of peasant scenes.

Plate II, 50. Jean-Léon Gérôme, *The Dog of Alcibiades*.
(Le chien d'Alcibiade.) Baron Martin Museum, Gray, France

A study ("painted from nature") for Alcibiades's dog in the 1861 painting *Alcibiades in the House of Aspasia* *(Alcibiade chez Aspasie).*[40]

Plate II, 51. Michelangelo, *Man Sitting on a Sack*.
(L'homme au sac.) Sistine Chapel, Vatican City

This drawing is after a figure in a fresco (1508–12) on the ceiling of the Sistine Chapel in the Vatican. The anatomy in the original is not totally correct, and the copy compounds Michelangelo's errors. The right shoulder and arm are exaggerated in size. Michelangelo's ability, however, comes through in the rhythmical disposition of the parts, which gives the body a sense of grace and movement.

Plate II, 52. Thomas Couture (1815–1879), *Portrait of a Young Boy*.
(Portrait d'un jeune garçon.) Whereabouts unknown

Couture had a distinguished career, although several large commissions from the French government remained unfinished because of the political upheavals during his lifetime. Known primarily for his large history paintings executed in a loose, individual style, he had many students, among them Anselm Feuerbach (1829–1880), Édouard Manet (1832–1883), William Morris Hunt (1824–1879), and Puvis de Chavannes.

Couture utilizes another manner of drawing the hair; compare it to the handling of hair by Henner (plate II, 17) and by Gleyre (plate II, 36). Couture uses long strokes of the charcoal for the general direction of the growth patterns and general veiling to indicate the top and lower planes of the head. Praiseworthy skill is evident in the drawing of the foreshortened ear, in the slight toning for the depression between the nasal bone and the nasal eminence, and in the gradual shading on the left cheek. The end of the nose has a planar quality, separating it from its sides.

Plate II, 53. Jules Lefebvre, *Head of a Woman.* *(Tête de femme.)* Whereabouts unknown

On Lefebvre, see comments to plate II, 34.

Plate II, 54. Timoléon Lobrichon (1831–1914), *Study of a Baby.* *(Étude d'enfant.)* Whereabouts unknown

Lobrichon was a student of François-Édouard Picot. In the 1850s he was associated with the Néo-Grecs, a group of painters, headed by Gérôme, who composed genre scenes set in antiquity. Later he painted mothers and children in modern settings.

This complete figure will aid you in understanding the difficulties of drawing babies, where baby fat and the surface bones dominate the shape and contours of the body and limbs. Note how the hair radiates from the crown of the head. Throughout outlines are strong, even in interior forms. The technique is similar to Holbein's in plates II, 19 and II, 60.

Plate II, 55. Hans Holbein the Younger, *Portrait of N. Poyntz.* *(Portrait de N. Poyntz.)* Collection of Her Majesty the Queen, Royal Library, Windsor Castle

The sitter is Sir Nicolas Poyntz. The plate is inscribed with an added signature *N. Poines Knight.*

Plate II, 56. Hans Holbein the Younger, *Portrait of Lady Hanegham.* *(Portrait de lady Hanegham.)* Collection of Her Majesty the Queen, Royal Library, Windsor Castle

Plate II, 57. Hans Holbein the Younger, *Portrait of the Wife of Jacques Meyer.* *(Portrait de la femme de Jacques Meyer.)* Öffentliche Kunstsammlung Basel, Kupferstichkabinett

Dorothea Kannengiesser and her husband, Jakob Meyer, the mayor of Basel, were drawn twice by Holbein, and the Kunstmuseum has both sets of drawings. This is from the second set and is dated 1525–26.

Plate II, 58. Hans Holbein the Younger, *Portrait of a Young Man.* *(Portrait d'un jeune homme.)* Whereabouts unknown

The style of this drawing is very close to that of Holbein's illustrious father, Hans Holbein the Elder (ca. 1465–ca. 1524). It may be an early drawing by the younger Holbein.

Plate II, 59. Hans Holbein the Younger, *Portrait of Lord Vaux.* *(Portrait de lord Vaux.)* Collection of Her Majesty the Queen, Royal Library, Windsor Castle

The sitter is Thomas, the second Lord Vaux.

Plate II, 60. Hans Holbein the Younger, *Thomas, Count of Surrey*.
(Portrait de Thomas, comte de Surrey.) Collection of Her Majesty the Queen,
Royal Library, Windsor Castle

The sitter is now identified as Henry Howard, earl of Surrey.

Holbein's naturalistic observations vie with the almost perfect oval of the face, as if he were subordinating nature to geometry. The faintly indicated clothing contrasts with the high finish of the face; individual strokes describe individual hairs; and the features of the face are very precise. Holbein is a master of the facial structure around the eye.

Plate II, 61. Philippe Parrot (1831–1894), *Bather*, study of a young girl.
(Baigneuse. [Étude de jeune fille].*)* Whereabouts unknown

Another "interpretation" of a painting. Now almost forgotten, Parrot specialized in portraits and elegant nudes in mythological guise.

Plate II, 62. Hans Holbein the Younger, *Portrait of a Man*.
(Portrait d'homme.) Whereabouts unknown

Before Word War II this drawing was in the collection of the duke of Weimar, in Weimar, Germany. The attribution to Holbein the Younger is not certain.

Plate II, 63. Hans Holbein the Younger, *Clinton*.
(Clinton.) Collection of Her Majesty the Queen, Royal Library,
Windsor Castle

The sitter is Edward, ninth earl of Clinton. Although the drawing is located at Windsor Castle by Goupil, it cannot be found in any catalogue of the collection.

Plate II, 64. Hans Holbein the Younger, *Portrait of a Lady*.
(Portrait de femme.) Whereabouts unknown

Plate II, 65. Hans Holbein the Younger, *Portrait of a Man*.
(Portrait d'homme.) Collection of Her Majesty the Queen, Royal Library,
Windsor Castle

Plate II, 66. Hans Holbein the Younger, *Lady of the Court of Henry IV*.
(Dame de la cour de Henri IV.) Öffentliche Kunstsammlung Basel,
Kupferstichkabinett

The sitter is Lady Guildford. This is a poor rendition of a masterful drawing by Holbein.

Plate II, 67. Hans Holbein the Younger, *Portrait of a Man*.
(Portrait d'homme.) Öffentliche Kunstsammlung Basel, Kupferstichkabinett

This is a sketch (1516) for one of the two paintings on panel of Jakob Meyer and his wife, also in the Kunstmuseum Basel (see comments to plate II, 57). In an extremely efficient manner Holbein has given much attention to the features of the face—such as the slight sag of the skin around Meyer's mouth and his chin—without detracting from the simplicity of the presentation. The clothing is simply outlined. In the finished oil it is painted from life. In the original preparatory drawing (see fig. 24) Holbein used silverpoint and red chalk.

Fig. 24.
Hans Holbein the Younger.
Portrait of a Man (Jakob
Meyer). *(Portrait d'homme.
Jacob Meyer.)* 1516.
Silverpoint and red chalk
on paper.
26.9 x 19.1 cm.
(10.5 x 7.5 in.)
Öffentliche
Kunstsammlung Basel,
Kupferstichkabinett.

PART III: PREPARATION FOR DRAWING *ACADÉMIES* (*EXERCICES AU FUSAIN POUR PRÉPARER À L'ÉTUDE DE L'ACADÉMIE D'APRÈS NATURE*)

INTRODUCTION

In general art-historical usage, an *académie* means a drawing or a painting of a nude model in a pose considered "noble and classic."[41] Highly finished charcoal drawings of male nudes were produced in such numbers in art academies that the institution became synonymous with its most representative product.

Female models were not used in life drawing classes at nineteenth-century academies until sometime after the middle of the century.[42] Students were expected to learn how to draw the female nude from statuary and other works of art, such as the models in the first and second parts of Bargue's *Drawing Course*. This was true even at the École des Beaux-Arts. Thus, the term *académie* in Bargue's title for the third part is the most restrictive use of the term: the seventy drawings are all of male nudes.[43]

The mastery of the nude male body was considered the most important part of the artist's repertoire, for it was taken for granted—in the persistent patriarchal worldview—that males were the most important members of society; for all practical purposes, they were also the most important characters in the historical and biblical subjects academy students were instructed to paint. Despite the fact that history paintings had gradually gone out of favor after the middle of the century—and that it had always been easier to sell a painting of a nude female than of a nude male—intense study of the male nude persisted until late in the nineteenth century. During the twentieth century the practice changed; now females are the favored models in art schools and drawing groups.

The results of the nineteenth-century practice can be seen in the works of Gérôme. In the lycée in his hometown of Vesoul there were no live models at all in any of the drawing and painting courses Gérôme took. When he left Vesoul and went to Paris in 1839, he studied in the ateliers of Delaroche and Gleyre; only the latter is known to have used female models, but Gérôme's time with Gleyre was a mere six months. Although his male nudes were, from the start of his career, both accurate and learned, it is easy to see from his early paintings that he had learned the female form by studying Greek statuary: his nude women are geometrically idealized, with taut skin over rounded forms, and with particularly firm, hemispherical breasts. Not until relatively late in his life—probably influenced by the growing severity of the standards of Realism—did Gérôme produce female nudes that seem to be drawn, painted, or sculpted from live models.

Ancient Sculpture as the Model of True Beauty: The Prevalence of Male Models

The nineteenth-century preference for male nudes as studio models had an old and embedded philosophical tradition behind it. The preference, nurtured and developed over a long period, was based on some tenets of Neoplatonism. The term covers a series of independent and different philosophical schools of thought in ancient and recent times, all sects or varieties of which were ultimately based on the dialogues of the ancient Greek philosopher Plato (427?–347 B.C.). Neoplatonism flourished, in various forms, into the seventh century A.D., when it was suppressed first by the Christians and then the Muslims as pagan, although many Neoplatonic ideas had already been assimilated by Christian theology. The interest of the humanists of the fifteenth century in ancient texts and philosophies led to a revival of Neoplatonic thought in several forms (such as philosophy, mysticism, and theurgy), branches of Neoplatonism that have influenced Western thought down through modern times. Popular astrology, for instance, is organized according to a Neoplatonic system: the planets are intermediaries between a higher, spiritual, reality and our world.

The belief by Plato that an independent, intelligible reality exists above and outside our sensible, material world is the basis of all schools of Neoplatonism. This higher reality is the realm of the truth, of values and principles that are the basis of our intellectual and moral life. The purpose of philosophy was the attainment of knowledge of these principles through study, instruction, ritual, revelation, and restraint of the senses (denial of the flesh). At the most elevated level it could result in a union of the individual soul with the highest sphere of the cosmos.

Human attainment of knowledge about the true principles was endangered by the lower emotions, which were aroused by the distracting sensory experience of the material world, or, as Christians saw it, a struggle between the spirit and the flesh. The sensory experience of this lower, material world evokes the lower emotions—lust, anger, gluttony, pride, envy, greed, sloth—which can consume our energies, weaken our judgment, and obscure the guidance of the higher principles, which already exist—instilled by God for our guidance—in our minds, thus delaying or destroying our ability to understand the true, absolute, and immutable principles or truths, such as piety, honor, obedience, justice, the Good, beauty, and so forth. To live an enlightened and blessed life, one had to free one's self from the domination of the senses, while clarifying to the point of unambiguous purity the concepts of the higher truths in our minds. Odd as it may seem, despite this antisensual argument, art—in particular the depiction of the nude human body—was seen as an aid in the pursuit of truth.

In Plato's dialogue *Phaedrus* the love for a beautiful youth is described as an aid to comprehending the higher principles of the mind. Even though love is evoked by the youth's physical beauty, the latter still provides an insight into the nature of true beauty, an insight that could lead to the knowledge of other absolute truths or principles planted by the creator in the mind but nonetheless difficult to access.[44]

It is important to stress that the path opened by physical beauty to true knowledge is also the path away from sensory or erotic entanglements. Giving in to the senses would not only debase the relationship of lovers but would further entangle them in the material world and obscure their understanding of higher principles. (Hence the popular expression "Platonic love.") Without embarrassment, this belief that falling in love could lead to spiritual enlightenments was revived by several Neoplatonists of the Italian Renaissance.[45]

The idealized male body, especially as exemplified in the sculpture of antiquity, became a paradigm of *true beauty*. This pagan association of virtue and beauty can be sensed in many ancient sculptures as well as in the works of the ardent Christian and fervent Neoplatonist, Michelangelo, as in his famous statue of *David* and his poetry.

In the eighteenth century Renaissance Neoplatonism informed the thought of Johann Joachim Winckelmann (1717–1768), the founder of archeology and a prolific writer on ancient art. While studying Greek sculpture, he decided that the beauty of the Greek depiction of male bodies was due not to idealization by Greek sculptors but rather to the perfect bodies of their models, the Greek men of antiquity. Moreover, these men were more beautiful than modern men because they were simply better people. The idea that the contemplation of natural male beauty opened the door to *la belle nature*—the pure and eternal idea of nature in the mind—and that this could lead to other higher truths remained popular into the second half of the nineteenth century.[46] Thus, through several manifestations the influence of Plato may be seen lurking beneath the exclusive use of male models in the École des Beaux-Arts until late in the nineteenth century, which is reflected in the third part of the *Drawing Course*.[47]

The ancient statuary of female nudes likewise presented women in an already idealized and ideal form. From the Renaissance on, most artists—docile, chaste, timid, or shy—used ancient statuary as models from which to learn how to pose females and how to depict their anatomy. In a pinch when dealing with a difficult pose, artists often used a male model—preferably slightly plump—to pose for a female figure; in addition to substituting a female head, they made a few bodily adjustments to feminize their drawing, such as adding breasts or thickening the hips. As the female nude began to predominate in Western art, its "rarefied beauty" and purity were praised; the simplification of natural forms through geometry, such as hemispherical breasts, represented a step toward the ideal, and hence toward moral thought.

Nonetheless, the counterargument—that viewing an image of a nude woman put the male viewer in moral peril of experiencing an erotic reaction or of harboring impure thoughts—was an important and persistent position. Thus, it was argued for centuries that both female and male nude bodies, if depicted, should be presented in an idealized manner, bereft of direct erotic stimulus. In France between 1875 and 1881 official censors inspected and approved prints and photographs of nudes before they could be put on public display or sold in shops. Despite this review, many approved prints and photos of nudes could not be displayed in shop windows. After 1881 the police were empowered to arrest those who made an offensive public display of a nude in a shop window, on a magazine or a book cover. If a trial ensued, the defense would usually argue that the nude, no matter how lasciviously depicted, was purified, with rounded, geometrical, unnatural forms—"like a sculpture"—and that the depiction was aimed at the higher consciousness and consequently was unlikely to arouse the lower emotions. The defense often won. In 1888 a lawyer defended a nude on the cover of the magazine *Le Courrier français* by pointing out that no genitalia were visible and that "the marmoreal bust with its imaginary rigidity and strength bears no trace of realism. . . . I see nothing more here than an admirably pure body, its lines powerful and chaste. . . ."[48]

Even so, students were thought to benefit in some practical sense from this philosophical preference for male nudes. Human anatomy was believed easier to grasp by observing the thinner, angular bodies of males than the fuller, rounder figures of females. It was thought easier to maintain discipline among the usually rowdy students—all male in most academies and art schools until very late in the nineteenth century—when the nude model was a male. Furthermore the teachers and administrators thought that they were protecting the morals of their students by shielding them from the power of the lower, sensual emotions that would be evoked by the depiction of a nude woman, especially one who was considered "available" (the popular assumption being that any woman who bared herself for money was of doubtful virtue). Even after the introduction of female models into the drawing classes in the mid or late nineteenth century, the general public, artists, and students often regarded and treated female models as no better than prostitutes.

Practical Matters: Copying the Drawings

As the title of this section indicates, these drawings of posed nude males are meant as preparation for drawing after live models in a studio. These exercises—the careful, exact copying of good drawings after a model—are meant to be executed in charcoal, as was the practice when drawing after a model posed in the studio. A good *académie* in charcoal should take at least fifteen hours, if not longer. Your copy should be developed and finished according to the steps in the first part (see the section entitled "Suggestions for Copying the Plates").

These *académies* are remarkable inventions of Bargue. You will come to appreciate them more and more as you work with them; your admiration will intensify when you start drawing from live models. Even so, the procedure—from schema to outline to shadows—was not Bargue's invention; it was standard practice in art schools and studios in the nineteenth century.

The drawings in this part are almost pure outline drawings, without shading or background; there are only sparse internal indications of anatomical features. Even if you are fairly advanced and sure of yourself, you should start out with the simpler, early plates, thereby making sure you grasp Bargue's procedural method.

The first two parts of the course were designed to make you see the essential elements of a figure and teach you a procedure for drawing from a model. The drawings in the third part stress structure and unity as opposed to seeing bodily parts separately. The large factors—character, pose, and proportion—are more important than surface detail. A quick perusal of the pages of the third part discloses just how little internal information Bargue puts within the outline: faces are left blank and hands and feet are often indicated by schematic lines. Furthermore, the complexities of the outline of the body are often reduced to straight lines between points, as in the first schemata for the cast drawings in the first part. Despite the fact that there is little internal musculature, the figures are both simple and successfully articulated.

As this is preparatory practice for drawing a nude from life, it is best to simulate the working conditions of drawing from a model in a studio. (In all the drawings in this part, the model is assumed to be on a platform at least 40 centimeters [16 inches] in height. This will put the eyes of a seated model about level with an artist standing at his easel—an ideal height for portraiture—and will result in the artist looking up at a standing nude.) This is best done by working with the Bargue *académie* and your drawing paper side by side or on a wall or on a straight (not angled) easel. (Students working without instructors should first carefully read appendix 2. Knowledge of sight-size practices will help students better understand many of the suggestions in the comments on the individual plates.)

At times the straight lines with which Bargue first captured the shape of certain parts of the body may seem like mannerisms, that is, traits or features reflecting a personal style; in practice these straight lines are tools that indicate the peaks of the planes on the surface of the body, which are demarcated by the protruding anatomical features under the skin. The straight lines do not retain their abstraction in the finished drawing, where they are usually rounded out to achieve a natural appearance. The schema—the resulting silhouette of connected outlines—is just the first step. And if you have worked through or from the plates in part I, you know how to proceed once you have outlined the figure. In part III only the last few drawings are finished: no shadow line has been developed and filled in and, of course, no halftones have been recorded. If you were working from a live model, you would be expected to finish the procedure, to produce a finished drawing with most of the surface modeled. Bargue teaches you to correctly draw the structure before you start adding the finishing touches, as well as how to determine the correct proportions of the outside shape of the subject; otherwise the interior features will not fit in correctly. You may continue making or checking your estimates by stepping back and measuring them at a distance; eventually you will make the measurements without a tool. Checking your drawing by comparing it with the model viewed in a hand mirror is always helpful.

With the Bargue drawing and your drawing side by side, you will soon learn to see errors. Remember, if these drawings were to be used as models for a painting, any inaccuracies would be compounded once you tried to fill in the interior. Such strictness is necessary both to teach you how to see and transcribe a human being's form correctly and to purge your own practice of any mannerisms or impreciseness that you may have already acquired.

The *Drawing Course* was published on full folio sheets, about four times as large as the reproductions in this book. If you are working in charcoal, you should take the book to a photocopy shop that has a good laser printer and have the drawing you wish to copy enlarged in color two or three times. It will be easier to see and understand Bargue's linear decisions in a larger drawing; many details would be virtually impossible to copy in a small scale, especially in charcoal. If you wish to copy directly from the book, you should work in pencil.

Some Notes on Bargue's Style

Bargue's use of straight lines seems intuitive rather than programmatic. In some complex anatomical areas (calves, knees, elbows, biceps, hands, and feet) he usually uses straight lines as a deliberate simplification. Whenever there is a lot of information to transcribe, the outlines of his forms generally tend toward straight lines. Just as often he uses a long, simple, sensuous and elegant line, slightly curved, taking in several dots. The virtuosity of these passages makes it seem as if he were performing for us, in comparison to the short, choppy units in the other passages.

The angles, both concave and convex, that change the contours of the figure imperceptibly are all based on internal anatomical features: swelling of muscles; attachments of tendons to bones; emerging surface bones; flexed muscles or fat. Emphasizing the protuberances of internal anatomical features punctuates the outline, clarifies the inner structure, and gives fullness to the contours. It takes a good knowledge of anatomy to see and articulate these features.

Bargue's abstraction of the figure involves more than the simplification of planes and outlines. Each of his figures has a singular rhythm that subordinates and subsumes the details—or, rather, unites them: each element supports the overall effect of the pose and the direction of the gestures.

Bargue uses overlapping lines to emphasize the structure of the body (as in plate III, 38). These lines assist in the foreshortening since they indicate if one form or muscle is in front of another. Bargue is particularly well versed in the construction of joints and the knee: he always indicates the patella, the protuberances of the condyles of the fibula and tibia, and the connecting tendons for the larger leg muscles that anchor themselves around the knee. Similarly, Bargue often records accented forms caused by folds in the flesh or pits like the navel, axillae, and the pit of the neck.

Bargue's indication of interior anatomy is almost calligraphic, particularly in the legs. These indications are drawn with a bit of brio. Some contours are quite refined, with Bargue recording all the expected changes in curvature (see the legs in plates III, 18, 19, and 37). Others are drawn in a more economical, "off the cuff" manner. For example, in plate III, 32 Bargue audaciously draws the outer contour of the left leg with a single sweeping arc that is interrupted only by the bend in the knee; in plate III, 41 the outer side of the right leg is a sinuous s-curve.

A Repertoire of Traditional Poses

In the many studies in part III Gérôme and Bargue have included a repertoire of traditional poses, some of which might occasionally have been useful to history or narrative painters. They were certainly useful to students at the École des Beaux-Arts in Paris, many of whom intended to compete for the Prix de Rome. A list of the recognizable poses follows.

Rhetorical poses: plates III, 10 and 37.

Allegorical figures: plates III, 28 and 40 (melancholy); plate III, 29 (grief or mourning [he could be holding an urn or a libation vessel]); plate III, 37 (prayer); plate III, 39 (grief); plate III, 47 (astonishment).

Action figures: plate III, 12 (David with his sling); plate III, 38 (an archer); plate III, 46 (a man tugging); plate III, 45 (stretching).

Famous figures: plate III, 24, Hippolyte Flandrin's *Young Man Seated on a Rock,* study *(Jeune Homme nu assis sur un rocher. Figure d'étude)*; plate III, 33, after Michelangelo's *Dying Slave (L'Esclave mourant)* (fig. 13); plate II, 35, the *Dying Gaul (Gaulois mourant)* at the Capitoline Museum in Rome.

Biblical figures: plate III, 12 (David); plate III, 15 (Saint John the Baptist or a shepherd); plate III, 18 (a shepherd); plate III, 36 (Adam expulsed from Paradise); plate III, 42 *(Ecce Homo)*; plate III, 44 (Abel dead, the dead Christ, or a martyr).

Traditional women's poses: plate III, 17 (examining a bird's nest); plate III, 50 (a bather).

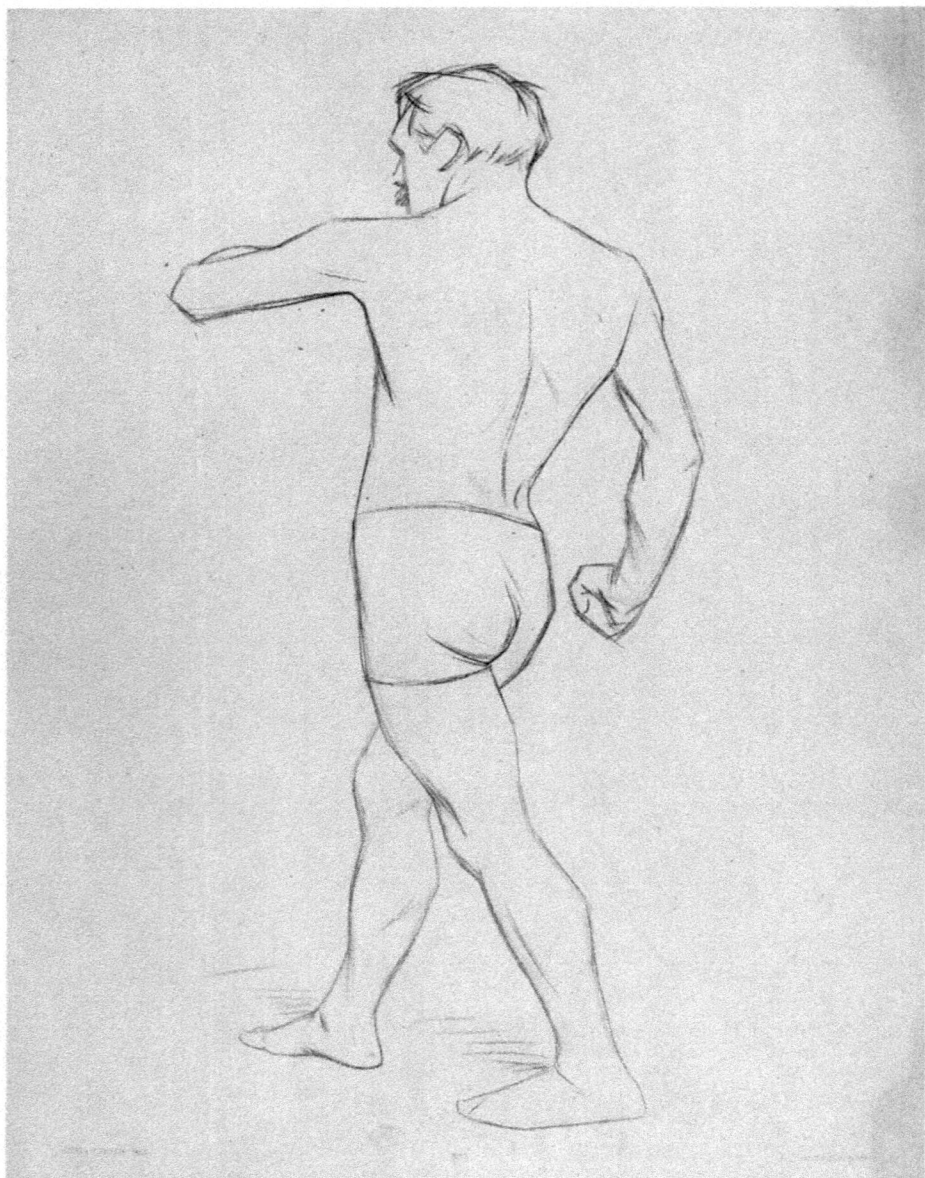

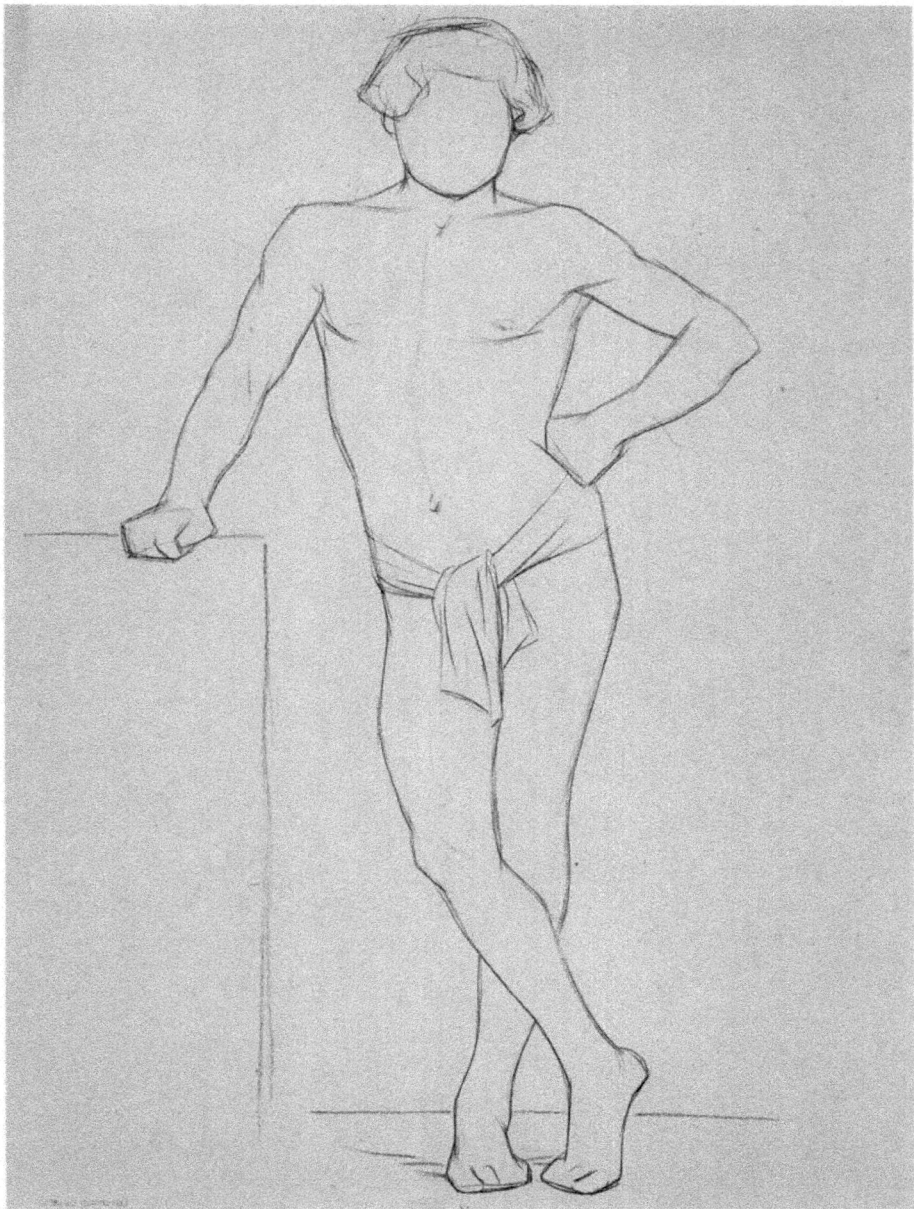

1.ᵉ Pᵗᵉ

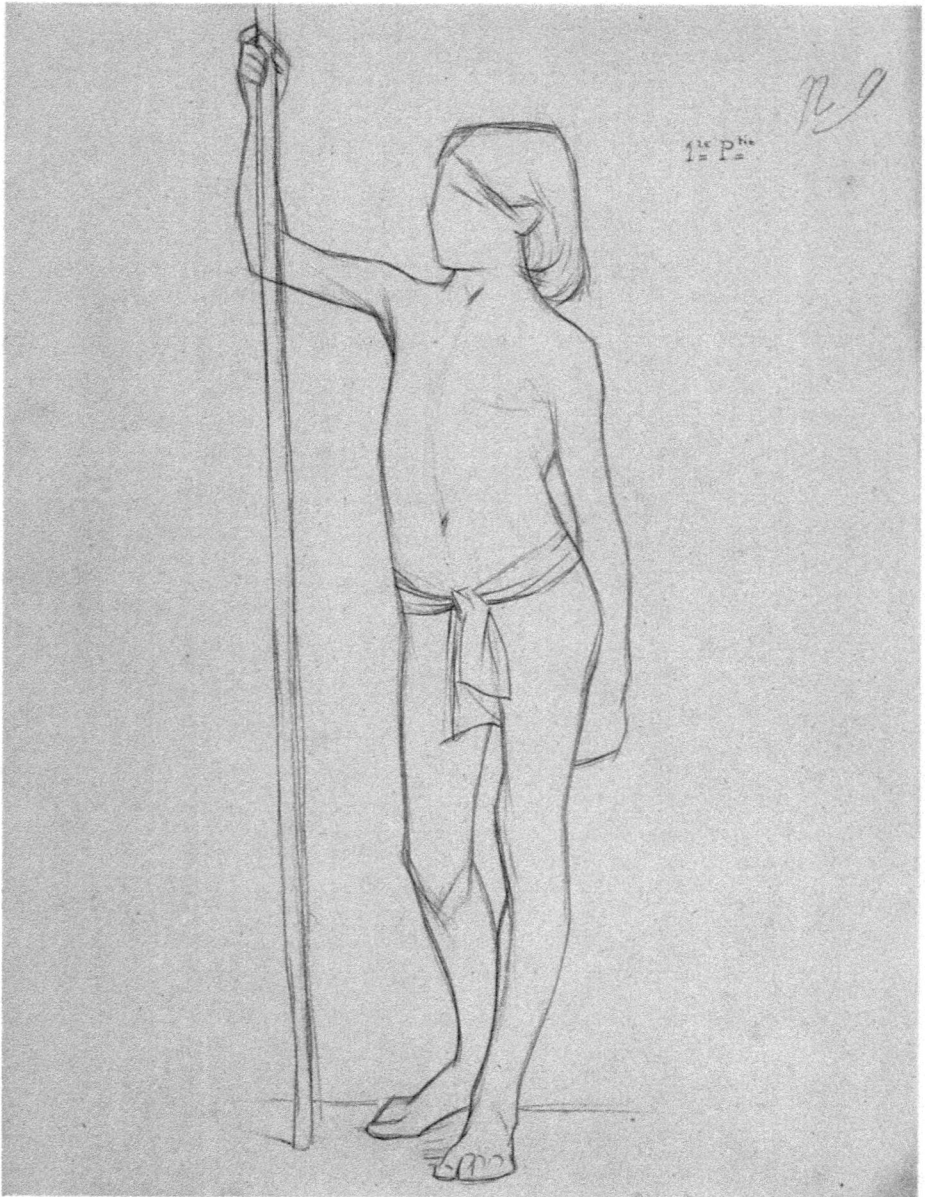

1ʳᵉ Pᵗⁱᵉ

129

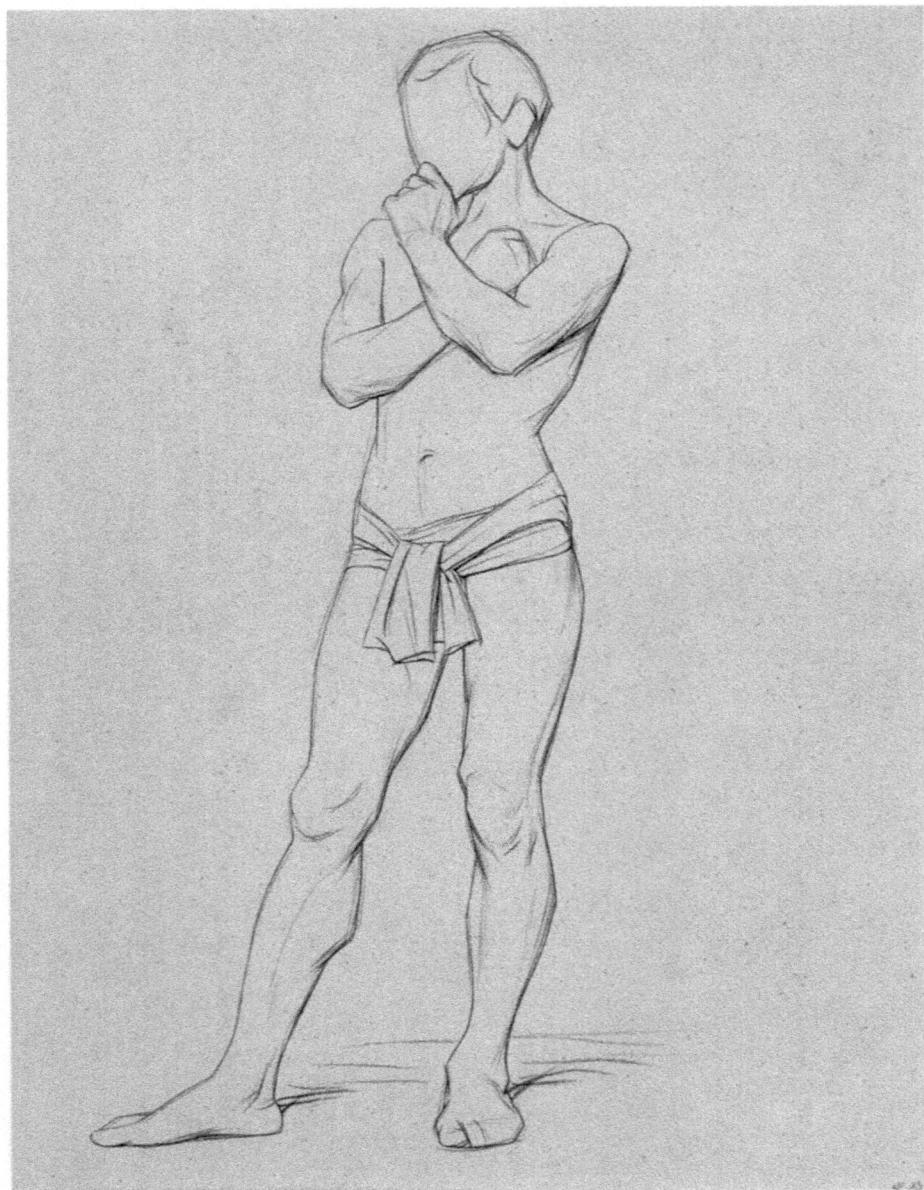

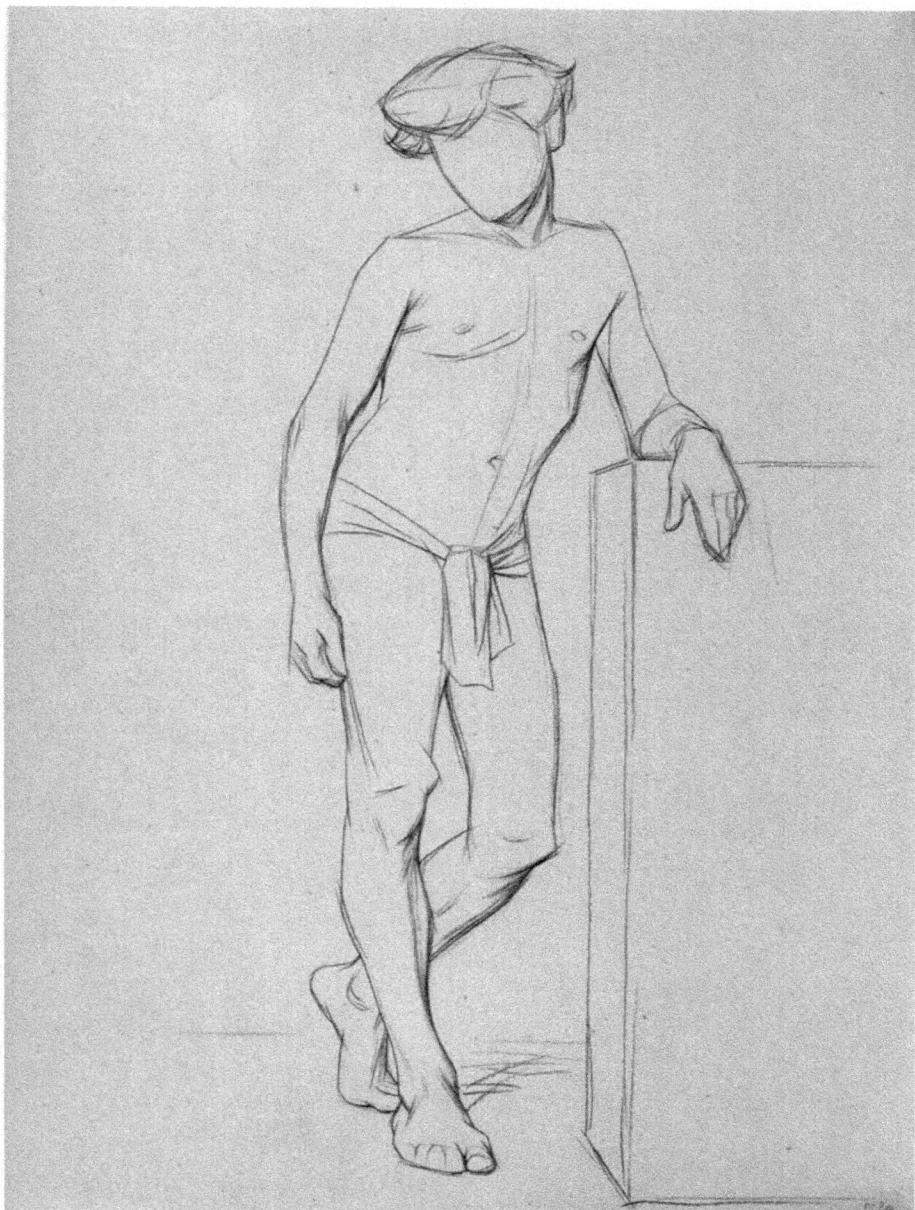

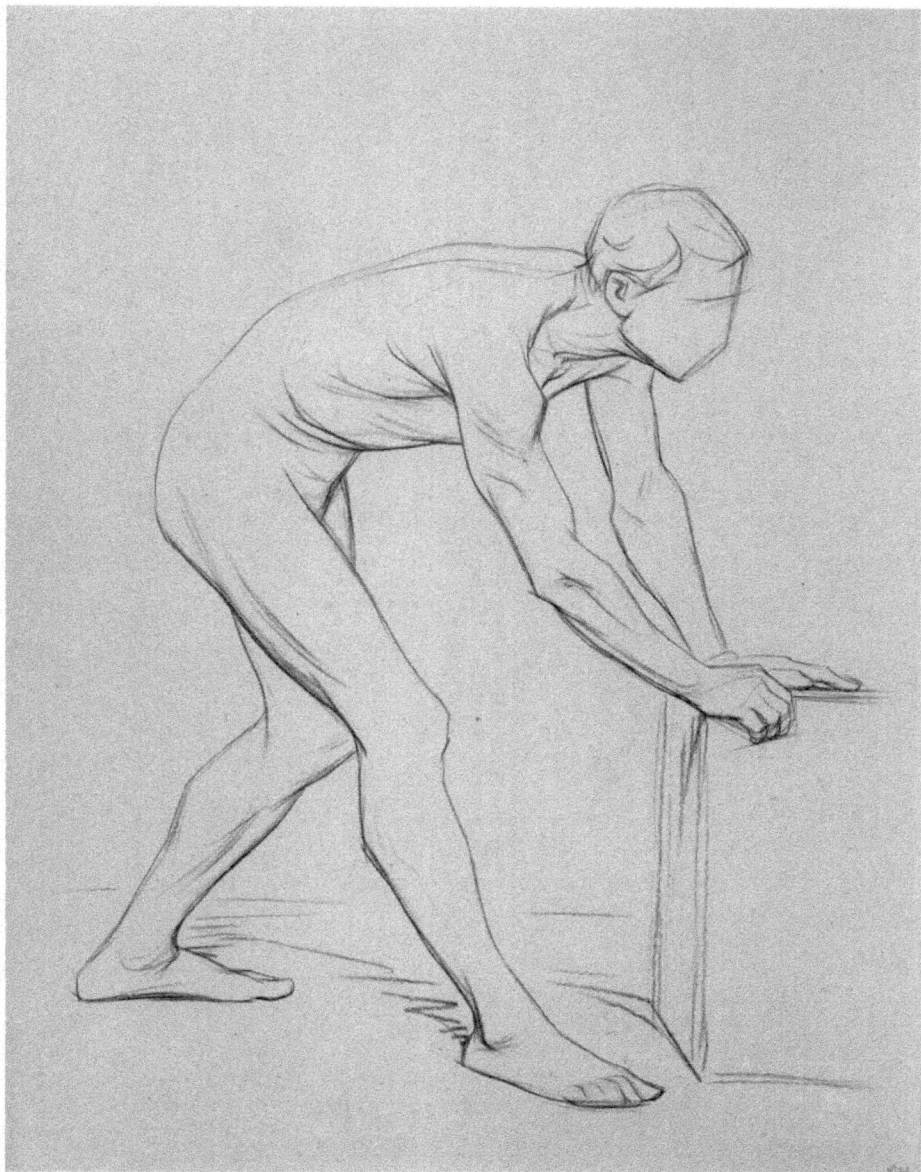

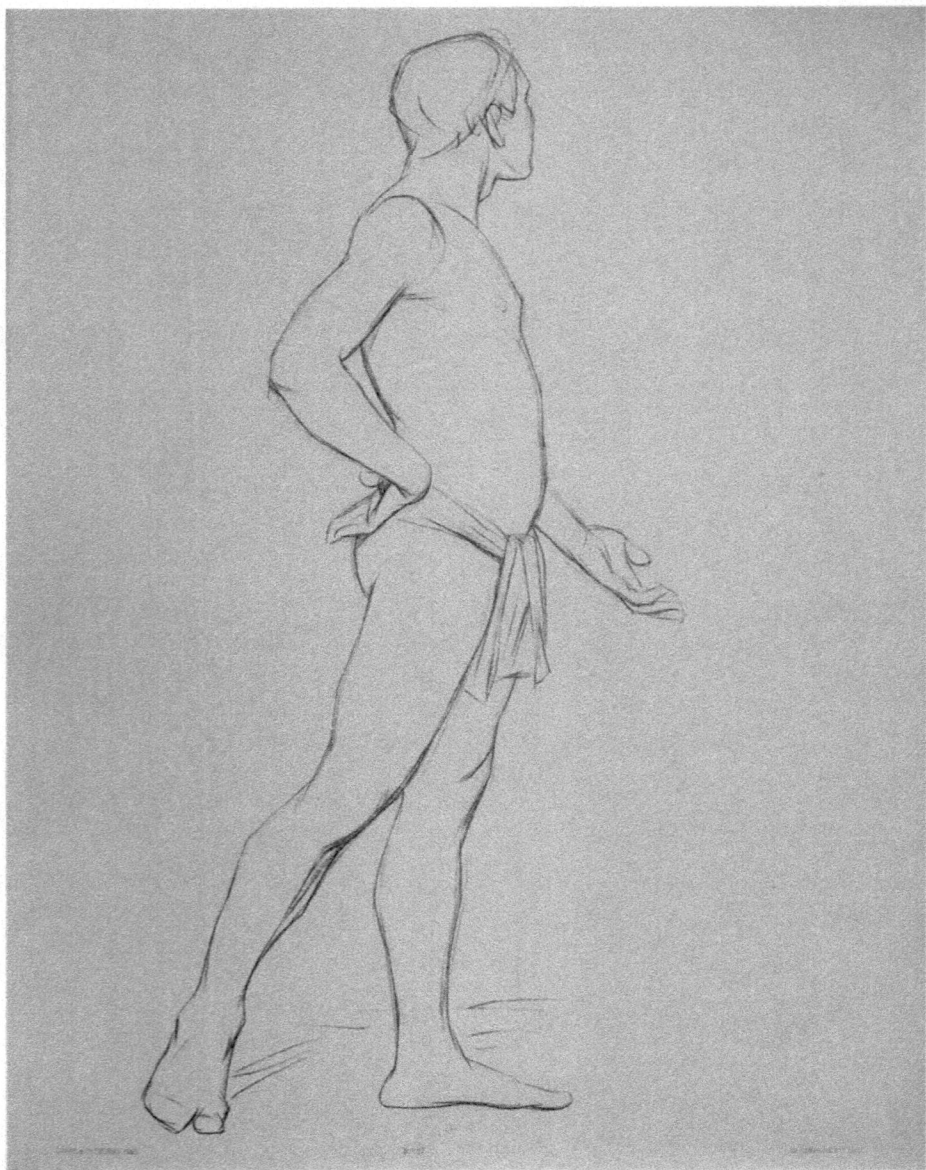

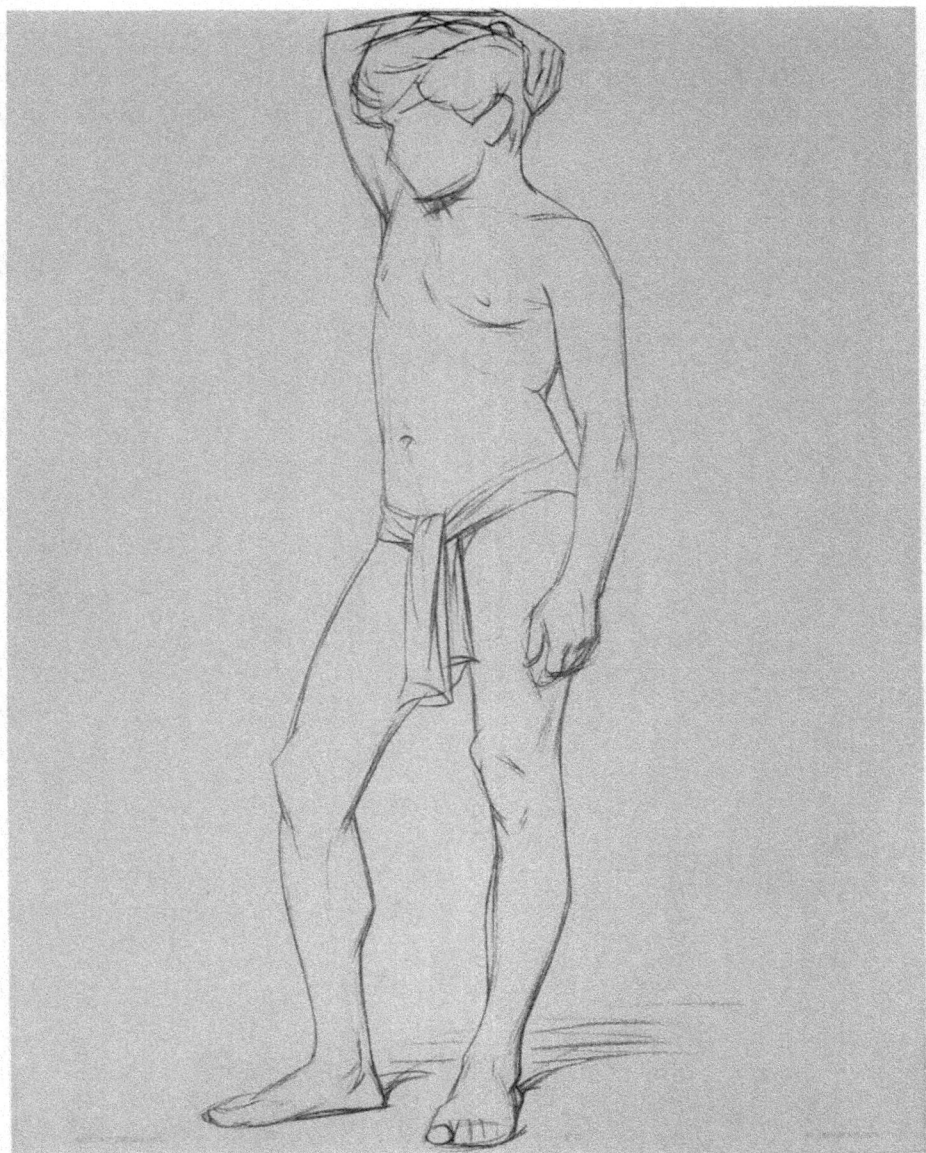

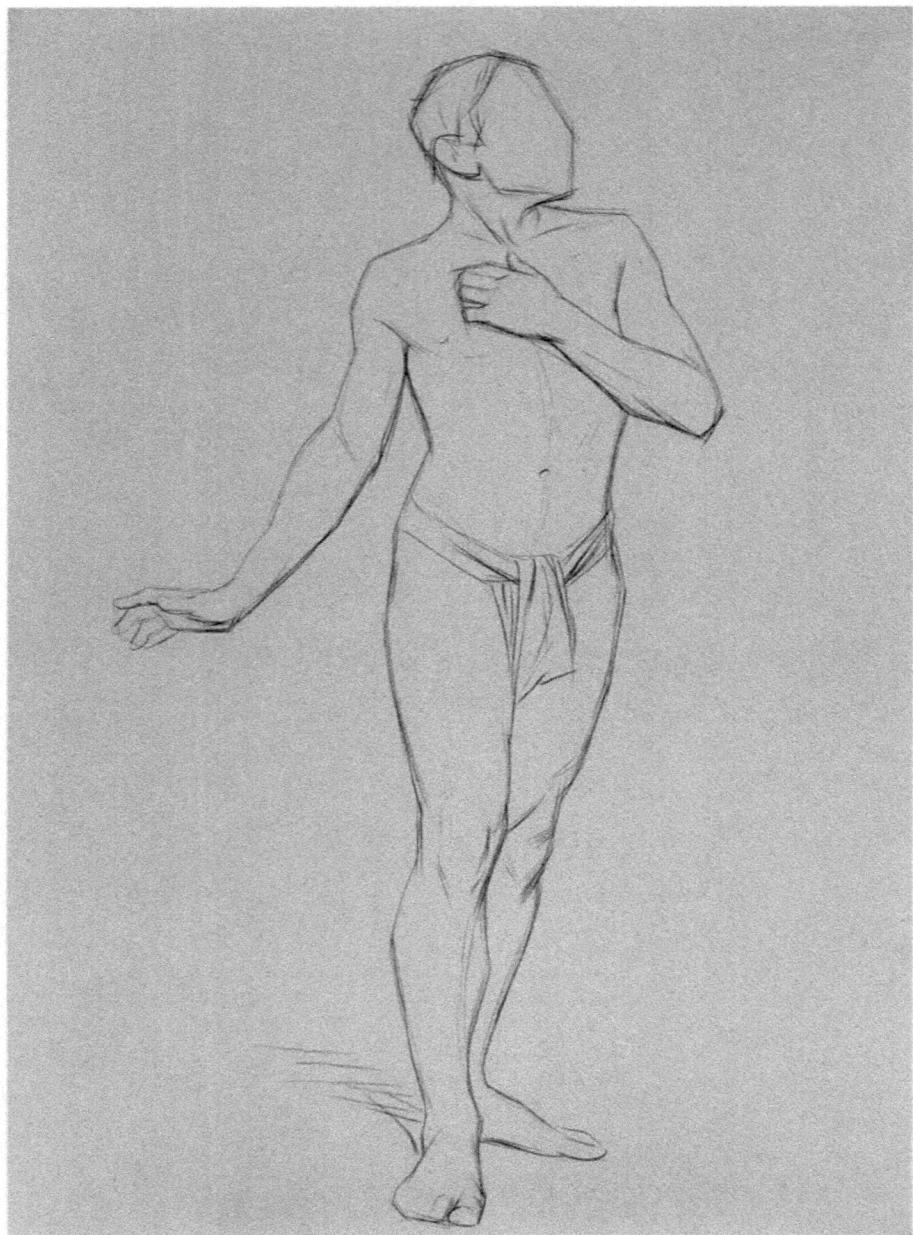

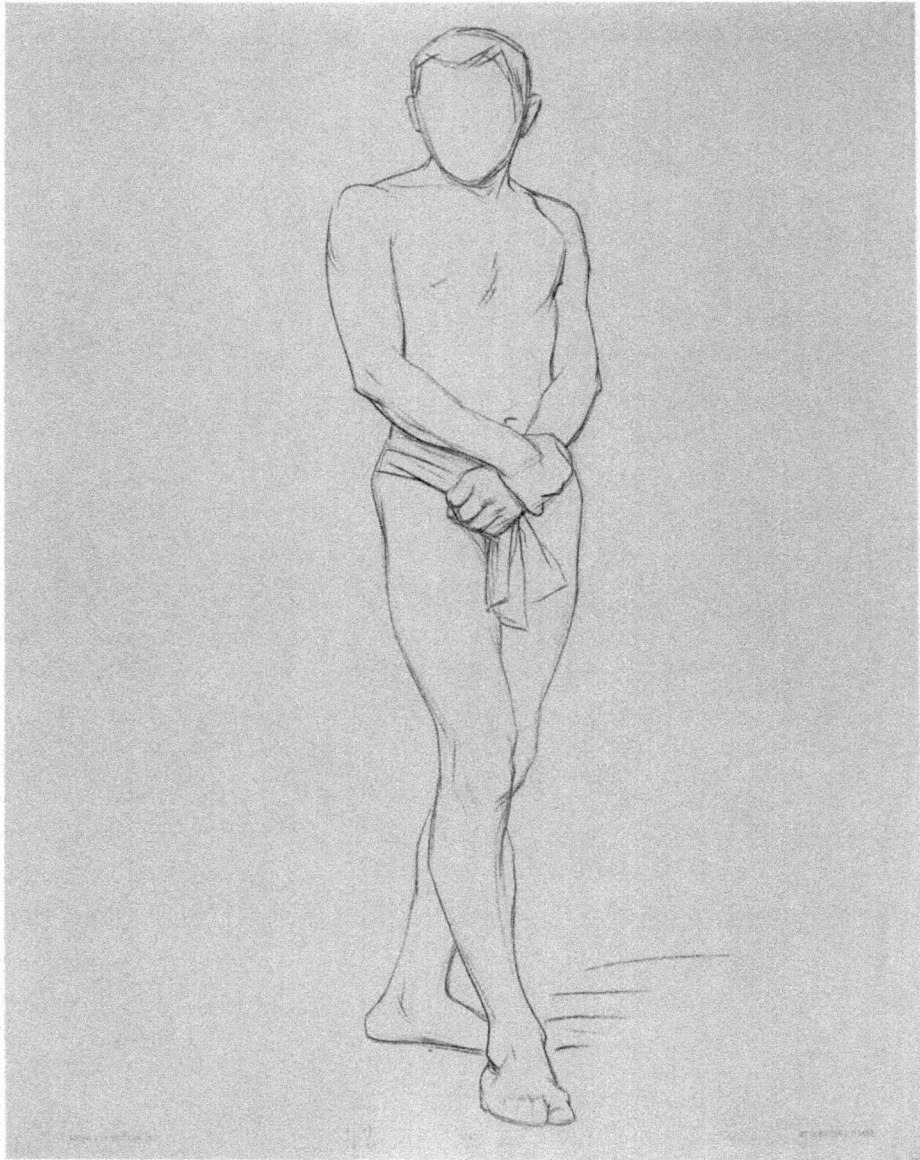

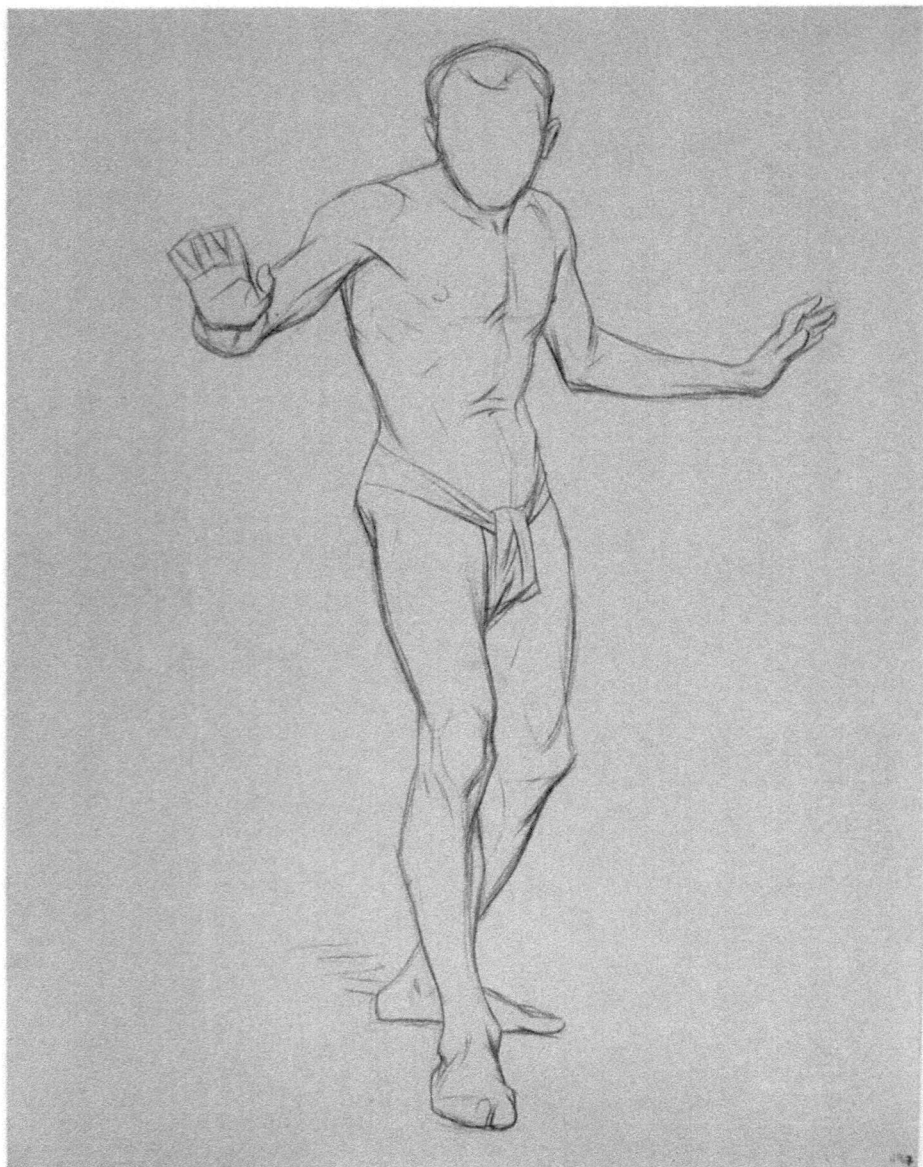

Plate III, 53

Plate III, 54

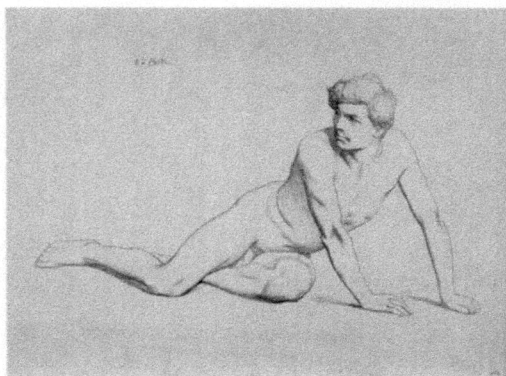

Plate III, 56

Plate III, 55

Plate III, 57

Plate III, 58

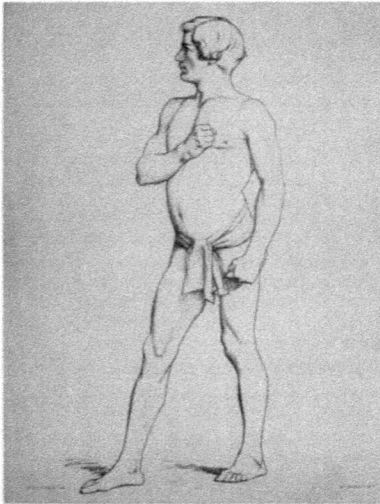

Plate III, 59

Plate III, 60

NOTES ON THE PLATES

[N.B.: The French titles used and translated are the modern inventory descriptions of the Goupil Museum. In the text "left" and "right" refer to the left and right side of the model.]

Plate III, 1. Young man, leaning on his right elbow.
(Jeune homme, accoudé sur le bras droit.)

The first drawing is the most simplified of all the figure drawings, reduced to an almost abstract figure of straight lines and angles; the emphasis is on proportion. Bargue wants you to begin the figure with straight lines right from the start. We suggest a plumb line from the bottom of the stand upon which the boy is sitting, through the margin of the stomach, and up the back of the neck. This is a popular, effective pose for a full-length portrait.

Plate III, 2. Young boy, standing while leaning on a box.
(Jeune garçon, debout accoudé à un mur.)

This is a funerary or mourning pose. The weight is divided between the feet and elbows. Pay attention to the very faint construction lines that travel between the buttocks and the upper body. *Note:* the line of the stand is an absolute vertical.

Plate III, 3. Standing man, walking, rear view.
(Homme debout, marchant, de dos.)

This drawing of a fighter is more developed than the previous two: the arms, the hair, and the shoulders are more detailed; the pose, with its many foreshortenings, is more sophisticated. In places the outline cuts into the body, following the shape of a muscle. These overlappings are one of the techniques Bargue teaches. The outer limits of the scapula are clear on his right side, while its inner limit is indicated inside the back. The bones of the elbows show through the skin. The lower part of the raised arm is drawn with two quick, overlapping lines. This is a pure outline, as if all the light were coming from the front, flattening the form. A light from a window or a lamp would cast a clear shadow across the body, as in most of the cast drawings in part I. The shadow line should be drawn first and then the shadow filled in with an even tone; the halftones may be added next. However, shadows are not recorded in most of the figure drawings of part III. I suggest a plumb line from the lower tip of the ear, through the knee, to the left toe. When drawing from nature—such as a studio model—it is best to make your first reference points from the bottom up. Although it does not make much difference when you are working from a drawing, you might start forming the habit of doing so now. With a model the position of the feet would be marked on the stand and would always be in the same place. The rest of the body will sway and move as the pose settles in. As a consequence, secure reference points taken from the feet will always be useful and assuring.

Plate III, 4. Standing young man, leaning on a box, front view.
(Jeune homme debout de face, appuyé sur un mur.)

This simple pose, with the emphasis on the outline, has only minor areas of foreshortening. There are some careful indications of anatomy in the upper body and arms. An important area is the interlocking of the model's left hand with the waist. In some areas you can guide yourself by the distances across empty spaces outside the figure, between limbs and the body (the so-called negative spaces). A good plumb line could run from the left side of his neck to the top of the little toe of the standing leg.

Plate III, 5. Standing young man leaning on a box while holding up his left arm, front view.
(Jeune homme debout, de face, appuyé sur un mur, levant le bras gauche.)

The model in this drawing was probably holding onto a pole or a rope suspended from the ceiling. There is tension in various parts of the body; pay attention to how this tension is shown and how it affects the anatomy. His right arm is very accurately foreshortened. Leaning on the box produces a tilt of the rib cage and gives an angle to the hips. An axis or medial line through the head and torso will help organize the proportions of the upper body; furthermore, the symmetrical features of the body will align themselves more or less perpendicular to the line.

Plate III, 6. Standing young man, leaning on a pole, left leg set back, side view.
(Jeune homme debout, de côté, appuyé sur un bâton, jambe gauche en arrière.)

This is a sensuous, serpentine pose with a surprising sense of movement initiated by the act of looking over the shoulder. There are broad and subtle overlappings along the back and shoulders. The plumb line can run from the right heel to the back side of the head.

Plate III, 7. Standing young man holding a pole behind himself in his left hand.
(Jeune homme debout tenant un bâton de la main gauche derrière lui.)

The young man could be pulling a sword out of a scabbard, albeit with his left hand. Concentrate on the rhythms of the muscles in the arm and legs. The plumb line runs from the part of his hair through his right foot.

Plate III, 8. Standing young man, right hand on his head, rear view.
(Jeune homme debout de dos, main droite sur la tête.)

The angles of the arms and legs are set in rhythmic response to one another. The main weight is on the left leg, although equilibrium is maintained by the right leg. The negative spaces are small but critical since they indicate that the legs are not touching. On the model's back Bargue uses predominantly straight lines to describe internal structure.

Plate III, 9. Standing young boy holding a pole, head turned toward the pole.
(Jeune garçon debout tenant un bâton, tête tournée vers le bâton.)

The only areas of pronounced foreshortening are in the legs and feet. The pole forms a safe negative space along the boy's right contour, which you can use to check your measurements and your shapes.

Plate III, 10. Standing man holding out his right hand, rear view.
(Homme debout de dos tendant la main droite.)

This could be the stance of an orator conceding a point (with his hand upturned); or it could be a repoussoir figure framing the central event of a history painting. The tension of the pose is described in several parts of the outline, particularly in the waist and thighs. The plumb line could run from the peak of the head to the inside right ankle.

Plate III, 11. Seated man, rear view.
(Homme assis de dos.)

After a popular studio pose, this is a more advanced, lifelike study. The outline is accurate, especially along the left side of the back, and the upper part of the leg. Light lines describe the medial line of the figure, and some of the internal structure. The weight of the body is emphasized by the flat line of the buttock and the bulging flesh above it.

Plate III, 12. Standing young man, right hand on left shoulder.
(Jeune homme debout, main gauche sur épaule droite.)

This could be the biblical David with his sling over his shoulder, getting ready to shift his weight forward (notice the tilt of the pelvis) for the pitch. The plumb line is from the peak of the head down. You may need vertical reference lines to assist you in plotting this narrow figure. In a free-standing pose the head is always positioned over the weight-bearing or standing leg (the other leg is sometimes referred to as the free or play leg).

Plate III, 13. Standing young boy holding a pole, legs crossed.
(Jeune garçon tenant un bâton, jambes croisées.)

The visible hand and the feet are drawn with great clarity and emphasis. Watch the proportions of the slightly foreshortened left arm. The pole steadies the model and furnishes an extra reference line from which to judge. This drawing also demonstrates that the head is usually positioned over the weight-bearing leg (although here it tilts slightly off center due to the support by the pole).

Plate III, 14. Standing young man turning his back, hands crossed behind him.
(Jeune garçon debout tournant le dos, mains croisées dans le dos.)

This could be a prisoner tied from behind. The angular outline stresses the boniness of the young body. There are obvious anatomical notations on the back, such as the scapulae, and more subtle ones on the legs, such as the tendons of the hamstring. The plumb line runs from the top of the neck to the inner right ankle.

Plate III, 15. Standing older man leaning against a stand while holding a pole.
(Vieil homme debout adossé à un mur tenant un bâton.)

The vague support—a wall or a stand—is clearly improvised; nevertheless sketch it in so that you will not forget how the weight is distributed in the stance. Observe how a faint line has organized the angles of the man's lower chest and belly. This observation relates nicely to the method taught in part I. Moreover, there are many negative spaces to help further organize the limbs. The plumb line runs from the peak of the head to the right toe.

Plate III, 16. Seated man, leaning on a wall.
(Homme assis, accoudé sur un mur.)

There are few straight lines in this splendid pose. The seated young man leans back against a table, so that all of the body recedes: the face is back, the hip forward. Study the position of the back and the upper torso. There are many good lessons in foreshortening in the drawing: one leg comes forward, the other goes back; the torso leans away from the viewer, the head is behind the shoulder; and the right arm reaches back, foreshortening the upper arm as well as the forearm.

Plate III, 17. Seated young boy, holding an object in front of him in his hands.
(Jeune garçon assis, tenant un objet devant lui dans ses mains.)

This is a moody pose, as if the boy were reading his fortune in a teacup. All the forms are lean and sinuous. His left leg, however, is in an inelegant view (a situation that often arises when models are carelessly posed and may be inevitable when many students work from the same model). Relate the right leg to the left as you draw.

Plate III, 18. Standing young man leaning on a pole.
(Jeune homme debout appuyé sur un bâton.)

This is a shepherd's pose. The young man is not so graceful as some of the other models; his legs are knobby and long. Pay attention to the articulation of the elbows and knees, which are described by Bargue with overlapping lines.

Plate III, 19. Standing young man, frontal view, with hand on chin.
(Jeune homme debout de face, main sur le menton.)

This could be either a pensive or pugilistic pose. Is he sizing up his opponent or simply dreaming? Although the model has articulated fingers, the toes are summarily indicated. The loincloth is elegant in that it does not obscure the silhouette. Part of each arm is in foreshortening. Study the marks that Bargue makes for internal features. Usually they describe the boundaries of major anatomical forms as well as the center lines of the torso. The plumb line runs from the right corner of the face to the inner ankle of the model's left foot.

Plate III, 20. Standing young boy leaning on a stand, left leg crossed behind the right leg.
(Jeune garçon debout accoudé à un mur, jambe gauche croisée derrière la droite.)

In this highly developed drawing, the arms, hair, shoulders, legs, and feet are all detailed. The pose is sophisticated; the parts of the body are arranged in interesting juxtapositions. Notice the overlapping of muscles on the legs. Carefully measure the foreshortening of the reclining upper arm. The several negative spaces can be used as guides to the shapes around them. Such sharp lines show the angles produced by the bones, whereas the softer lines show muscle and fat.

Plate III, 21. Seated young man, three-quarter view, hair somewhat long.
(Jeune homme assis, trois quarts, cheveux mi-longs.)

The slump of the torso is shown by curves, the boniness of the arms and legs by straight lines. Bargue's main interest is in the upper body, particularly in the tension of the supporting left arm. The plumb line runs from the peak of his face to the side of the box. This helps in measuring the distance from the box to the left toe, and so forth. In addition to a plumb line, extra horizontal reference lines (all perpendicular to the plumb line) would help to organize the various areas, say, through the top of the box under the buttocks and through the navel and left elbow.

Plate III, 22. Man in profile, leaning to the right.
(Homme de profil, penchant à droite.)

This is a pose with some action or movement indicated. It is a successful drawing, especially in the forms of the two arms. It is important to transcribe the negative spaces accurately. The tension between the left and right side of the contour is subtle and sensitive; small deviations in the contours may detract from the roundness of the figure. Work from side to side across the form and notice the variety of the contours. Normally a depression on one side will be paired with a swelling on the other. Again, some well-placed horizontals will help divide the figure into manageable areas.

Plate III, 23. Standing man, right hand on a stand.
(Homme debout, main droite posée sur un mur.)

In this classic pose the head tilts back with a hopeful expression. The left knee is locked to indicate support and the belly protrudes forward gently, adding grace and movement to the pose. You need horizontals here as well as a plumb line.

Plate III, 24. Man seated upon the ground, his head on his knees.
(Homme assis sur le sol, tête sur les genoux.)

The youth in this splendid drawing holds a pose similar to that in the famous painting of 1836 by Hippolyte Flandrin entitled Young Nude Boy Seated by the Sea, study (Jeune homme nu assis au bord de la mer. Étude), in the Louvre Museum in Paris. The areas of greatest interest are his right arm and hands, the vertebrae on the back of the neck, and the blocky feet. You'll need horizontals as well as a plumb line to organize your work.

Plate III, 25. Standing man, seen from behind.
(Homme debout de dos.)

A back view is always difficult because of the ever-changing morphology of bones, muscles, and fat. This is an older model, and the muscles and fat under the skin have sagged in a few places. The weight displacement is on his left leg, throwing the left hip up and the right one down. The foreshortened right foot is obscured, making it difficult to copy. You have to measure the angle of the foot from a horizontal. Bargue's attention to structure and the shift of bodily weight is as refined as his subtle notations of age. This drawing is a splendid example of the mixture of the idealist and realist interests of the Academic Realists.

Plate III, 26. Standing young man, holding a pole in his left hand while looking at it.
(Jeune garçon debout, tenant un bâton de sa main gauche et le regardant.)

This is a well-developed drawing with accurate proportions. The gesture is subtle: the boy looks up toward the pole in his left hand (as if he were admiring a banner lost to our view); he shifts his weight to the right leg, and moves his left leg back. As a result, his shoulders and hips tilt at opposing angles. Opposing angles similarly animate the fingers, which are carefully arranged on his left hand.

Plate III, 27. Standing man, in profile, holding out his open left hand.
(Homme debout de profil tendant la main gauche ouverte.)

This subtle drawing emphasizes the placing of the weight on the model's left leg. The head is clear in its turn and structure. The hand bent back by the akimbo arm is noteworthy; the other hand—held in a position that a model would find hard to maintain—seems to have given Bargue trouble. This hand appears to have been added later; its gesture is not supported by any connection with the body, which inevitably makes it look too large. Such an effect was perhaps unavoidable given this pose. The classical rule is to choose a view in which all major joints are visible.

Plate III, 28. Young man seated on a box, his right hand supporting his head.
(Jeune garçon assis sur une caisse, main droite soutenant la tête.)

Traditionally a cheek resting on the hand of a seated figure represents melancholy. The most famous examples are Dürer's 1514 engraving Melancholia I and Rodin's 1880 statue The Thinker (Le Penseur). Melancholy is one of the traditional four humors (or temperaments) that determine human physiognomy and personality. The humors were an integral part of the Neoplatonic system; even today they are embedded, albeit discreetly, in popular astrology. The emphasis is on the supporting left arm; notice the taut deltoid and scapula. Faint construction lines are visible throughout, and there are indications of the ulna and patellae. The hand is carefully blocked out to show its importance and to balance it with the foreshortened arm and hand holding up his head. Use horizontal reference lines as needed.

Plate III, 29. Young man in profile holding a ball.
(Jeune homme de profil tenant une balle.)

The figure holds a ball, putting the biceps of the arm in flexion to support the weight; the tension runs down the right side of the body through the locked knee. The far side of the body, not bearing the weight, is relaxed and lowered. The entire torso from buttock to neck is exemplary. The chest, belly, and thigh are described by a single curved line.

Plate III, 30. Standing man in three-quarter view, holding a pole with both hands, his left leg crossed over the right.
(Homme debout de trois quarts, tenant un bâton à deux mains, pied gauche croisé devant le pied droit.)

This drawing of a mature man with fairly well developed anatomy emphasizes gesture and movement. Compare him with other models, such as in plate III, 33, and note how his contours differ from the younger men. The right foot seems to be an undeveloped thought.

Plate III, 31. Seated man in profile, his hands crossed on his left knee.
(Homme assis en profil, les mains croisées sur genou gauche.)

This is an excellent example of a well-proportioned figure with judicious indications of anatomy. The negative shapes are clear and therefore helpful. The foremost leg is accurately drawn. The arms are twisted over one another. Make sure you pay attention to the rhythms in the outlines of the legs and arms by precisely placing the high and low parts of their curves, all the while comparing one side of the contour to the other. Draw the left and right sides at the same time, using the internal indications of anatomy to guide you.

Plate III, 32. Standing young man, right arm resting on his head.
(Jeune homme debout, bras droit posé sur la tête.)

When copying this model remember that the two legs are on different planes!

Plate III, 33. Standing man, right hand on his chest, left hand on his head.
(Homme debout, main droite sur le poitrine, main gauche sur la tête.)

The model imitates the pose of Michelangelo's *Dying Slave* (*L'Esclave mourant*) in the Louvre Museum in Paris (studied in plate III, 30 and shown complete in fig. 13). The view is higher than in the other drawings. Notice how the feet steady the body, as if he were standing on an incline. Be sure to maintain the character of the model's maturity throughout the drawing; his limbs are thicker and more muscular than those of a youthful body. The drawing of the right arm and of the right leg is noteworthy.

Plate III, 34. Standing young man, turning his head to the left, right hand extended.
(Jeune homme debout, tournant la tête vers la gauche, main droite tendue.)

This very exciting drawing combines the subtlety and grace of the *contrapposto* pose with an extended, foreshortened, and accurately viewed right arm. It exemplifies several qualities of a good drawing, combining an interesting pose, a legible mood, clear anatomy, and a simplified line.

Plate III, 35. Half prone man, holding himself up on his hands.
(Homme presque allongé se soutenant de ses bras.)

The pose echoes that of the famous *Dying Gaul* (ca. 190 B.C.) in the Capitoline Museum in Rome. Each arm bears weight in a different manner. The foreshortened legs must be copied exactly. Throughout, the information—external and internal—is very subtle. The boy was probably first inscribed within a triangle of construction lines, with a plumb line through one side of the head and left hand. Try to imagine such geometrical shapes around your figures as you were trained to do in the cast drawings (see comments to plate I, 5).

Plate III, 36. Standing man in profile, hiding his face in his hands.
(Homme debout de profil, se cachant le visage dans les mains.)

The pose is for Adam being expulsed from Paradise; it is a rhetorical pose, with codified gestures. It could be used for anyone in despair or grief. Throughout this section Bargue helps the student develop a repertoire of archetypal poses. Learn to distinguish their individual qualities; consider how figures can communicate meaning and emotion.

Plate III, 37. Standing man, left hand on his chest, right hand extended.
(Homme debout, main gauche sur la poitrine, main droite en arrière.)

The man strides forward, looking up as if imploring someone and putting his hand on his chest to demonstrate his sincerity. Note the grace of the extended arm and the carefully posed fingers. This pose is traditional and, although rhetorical, it is full of emotion. The fact that a pose is traditional does not mean it is worn out and useless; a good artist can infuse standard iconography with fresh expression by rethinking and experiencing the emotion, resulting in a figure that is legible and communicative.

Plate III, 38. An archer.
(Homme tirant à l'arc.)

This drawing emphasizes the archer's balance and the muscular tension throughout his body —especially in his arms and upper body—as he pulls the bowstring back.

Plate III, 39. Seated man, hiding his face in his hands.
(Homme assis, se cachant le visage dans les mains.)

The student must learn to draw the figure in a variety of poses—seated, lying down, leaning—with each position presenting specific problems. This pose is complex, containing more detailed observation than hitherto. Be careful to preserve the relationship of height and width so that the negative spaces retain their descriptive quality. Also pay attention to the breaks and overlappings in the contour.

Plate III, 40. Standing man, right hand on his chin, left hand behind his back.
(Homme debout, main droite sur le menton, main gauche dans le dos.)

Since antiquity the gesture of the hand to the chin has traditionally symbolized pensive contemplation. Among the problems that should be noted, the arms are both rather cumbersome in their foreshortening. Although the right arm is well drawn, the left elbow seems out of place. The upper torso looks small relative to the hip, legs, and head. Assume this pose and check the appearance of your arms in a mirror, or ask a friend to assume the pose for you. The rhythms of the legs are well conceived and the disposition of weight seems logical.

Plate III, 41. Standing young man, left hand resting on a stand, right hand akimbo.
(Jeune homme debout, main gauche posée sur un mur, main droite sur les reins.)

This is an assertive pose. The young boy stands alongside the box, with one hand resting on it. Between the weight of the hand on the box and the weight on his standing leg, an equilibrium is established which resounds throughout the body. The concavity of his right side emphasizes the jut of the pelvis and then quickly turns into the convexity of the buttock. A good plumb line would run down the center of his body, from the pit of his neck through his navel. Note how many straight notations have been turned into curves.

Plate III, 42. Standing young man, hands crossed over his waist.
(Jeune homme debout, mains croisées sur le ventre.)

Here is another bound prisoner, this time with his arms in front. This could also be Christ, either presented to the populace in the traditional *Ecce homo* iconography, or being baptized by John the Baptist. The drawing is a good example of anatomical articulation, particularly in the legs around the knees and calves.

Plate III, 43. Man leaning against a stand, face lifted up.
(Homme appuyé le long d'un mur, visage vers le haut.)

This is a very relaxed pose seen from a low position. The legs are strong, the fingers nicely posed and spaced, and there are great subtleties of observation in the outline of his left side, from shoulder to groin. Note the depiction of his weight-bearing right hand.

Plate III, 44. Supine young man.
(Jeune homme allongé.)

A supine young man with foreshortening effects across his whole body. This is a pose often used for the dead Christ, the dead Abel, and various martyrs. Use vertical reference lines to divide the body into manageable portions; for example, from the ends of the fingers of the right hand up through the thighs. Continue relating one part of the body to the other.

Plate III, 45. Standing man, his hands behind his head, looking up.
(Homme debout, mains derrière la tête, visage en haut.)

This is a wonderful drawing of a man stretching. The relatively low placement of the ears assists the foreshortening of the head. Muscular rhythms play throughout the body. Very light interior lines show features of the anatomy, such as the under part of the chin. On both sides you can see the insertion of the latissimus dorsi into the armpit. The left leg is seen from the medial angle, that is, from the inside, and should be much wider than the right leg, seen from the front, which it is not.

Plate III, 46. Man pulling on a rope.
(Homme tirant une corde.)

This drawing depicts a man—with a rather small head for his body—pulling on a rope. The gesture suggests that he is pulling against someone. The right pelvis has dropped and the left buttock is compressed as a result of the physical effort. The tapering of the right bicep into the forearm is precisely noted. In drawing an action, pay attention to the muscles that are working. They contract and change their forms: muscles are shorter and fuller in flexion and leaner and longer in extension.

Plate III, 47. Standing man, arms spread out.
(Homme debout, bras écartés.)

This pose could represent surprise or astonishment. This is a very developed drawing even without a face. Notice the guiding schematic lines of the hands: Bargue groups the fingers together rather than drawing them individually. This example provides an extremely good drawing lesson: you see indications of the sternum, the knees, and the ankles. Bargue does not want you to forget where the bones are. He has caught the movement of the figure in all the limbs. Note the foreshortening of the right forearm and of the left upper arm. Academies in the nineteenth century usually had ropes hanging from the ceiling to help the models maintain such poses.

Plate III, 48. Standing young man, three-quarter rear view, crossed arms.
(Jeune homme debout, trois quarts de dos, bras croisés.)

This drawing shows a bystander in pensive mood. The young man has fine legs, broad buttocks, and faintly defined shoulder muscles. From this point on the facial features are included, and the internal anatomical features are better described than in previous examples.

APPENDIX 2: The Sight-Size Technique

An Experienced Artist and Teacher Defines the Sight-Size Technique

In the course of a letter exchange about the sight-size technique, Peter Bougie, who has been teaching the procedure to his students in his Minneapolis, Minnesota, atelier for years, sent me this fine explanation of the technique:

> The sight-size method of measurement was a common method of working for both students and accomplished artists prior to the twentieth century, during which it fell into disuse in most art education settings. The term "sight-size" refers to making a drawing the size it would be if projected onto a plane extending left or right from your drawing board and intersecting your line of sight. This enables the artist to look at the subject and the drawing from a chosen vantage point and see them side by side—and appearing to be the same size. A plumb line [see glossary] is established for measuring widths on the subject from an established point, and a hand-held plumb line is used to line up features of the subject with the corresponding features of the drawing. This enables the artist to make very objective, virtually absolute, comparisons of shape and proportion. It is a superlative learning tool because it helps the student see objectively how what he or she has done compares to nature; that is, is the knee too high or too low? Has the width measurement to the end of the nose been placed too far from the vertical plumb line or too near to it? If you want the answer to either question, pick up the plumb line and see for yourself. The technique is an excellent tool because it establishes a common vantage point, an objective point of view, between student and teacher. There is no place for arguments about relative point of view, for the teacher and the student look at the subject from the same point of view, and the teacher is able to point out errors and incorrect observations objectively, and so help the student to see and understand what is really there, instead of offering vague generalities about whether or not something feels right or wrong. Finally, it is an excellent working method for any artist who wishes to use it in working directly from life in a controlled setting, because once you have mastered it you are able to fix solid reference points on a drawing or painting quickly, and save yourself a lot of misapplied effort. . . . Sight-size is a well known and proven method for taking measurements in a setting where the model is posed, or the subject is stationary. It's a tool. It is no more theoretical than a pencil or a paintbrush. It's useful when it's used in the right way. Above all, the sight-size method is used to help students develop and improve their "eye" and, as they advance, their problem-solving skills.

Using Sight-Size to Copy the Bargue Plates

The use of sight-size technique is recommended in all three parts of the course. It is basically a method of drawing in which the image produced has the same dimensions on paper as the apparent dimensions of the subject. There are several advantages to this technique when it is followed correctly. It produces an accurate transcription of the subject in the same size in which it is perceived. This permits continuous comparison of the drawing with the model. Once students have become proficient in the use of sight-size, they can easily correct their own work. The practice of the sight-size technique also increases a student's ability to estimate accurately the apparent measurements of the subject and transfer them correctly to paper. This talent soon becomes instinctive; it is the greatest gift of practicing sight-size. Both abilities—being able to correct oneself and being able to estimate measurements—give the beginning student a sense of confidence. For beginners, the advantages of the sight-size technique are so great that it is recommended here, especially for students working alone. Although intended for drawing from nature, that is, from three-dimensional objects, it is easily adapted to the copying of drawings. Using sight-size technique would standardize the approach to all three tasks presented in the course (viz. working from casts, copying drawings, and drawing académies) and, in general, would be a proper preparation for the first drawing from live models using the technique.

How Old is the Technique?

There is endless debate among the practitioners about how old the technique is and about who practiced it. Some adherents have attempted to resurrect an ennobling lineage of artists who used the method, much like Renaissance dukes and popes extending their family trees back to Hercules. As a methodical studio practice it seems to be a late nineteenth-century development. Although there are many instances where one unself-consciously uses it not as a method but as a natural approach—say, in portraiture or capturing figures at a distance—it is best as an atelier practice. The examination of many etchings, drawings, paintings, and photographs of early ateliers in session—some as far back as the Renaissance—depict none of the upright easels necessary for the practice of sight-size. In many other depictions of older ateliers, one constantly sees younger students seated on the ground, with their drawing boards in their laps.[82]

Necessary Conditions for Sight-Size Practice

First, the object drawn and the paper upon which the object's appearance is transcribed must remain stable. Also, the drawing board on the easel must be precisely upright and the easel stable—in the same position on the floor—for the entire time the drawing takes to complete, which may be several weeks. The light upon the object should always be a stable, directional, light or, if coming from a window, always from the same northern exposure. This means that the space or room must maintain the same setup until the drawing is finished.

Second, the observing position of the artist as he or she studies the object and the drawing must always be the same. The observing position is usually at a comfortable distance from the setup and the easel, say, three times the largest dimension of the drawing (to reduce the angle of distortion) and at a spot where the drawing paper and the subject are visually side by side.

Mark the position of your feet on the floor with tape, indicating the position of each foot. The feet are best planted at shoulder-width distance from each other; this increases your steadiness. Plant your feet in position, lock your knees, and stand up straight each

Fig. 44.
The Shadow Box
Left: the setup of the box with a cast.
Right: floor plan of setup indicating the marked, working foot position.
Drawing. Graydon Parrish

time you step back to observe the subject or the drawing. Wear the same shoes throughout the drawing process. Even the slightest change of view—such as higher or lower heels—can affect your view and your judgment.

Note: Never draw the object while looking directly at it; always study it from the same place and distance, and draw from memory, aided by your measured marks.

Excursus: Shadow Boxes

A shadow box is usually used for cast drawings. You will be copying from drawings already made from a cast. Even so, it is good to know how these cast drawings were made since this will help you when you switch from the Bargue cast drawings to actual casts.

The shadow box used for the cast setup is a small, three-sided box with a bottom but no top, and two adjacent vertical sides. It can be built from scratch or reconstructed from a wooden box (see fig. 44). The box, of course, rests on a solid stand or table that elevates it to easel height, so that when you stand in position you are looking at the center of the object. Line the box with black paper or cloth to absorb light and thereby lessen reflected shadows on the cast. (Some users prefer a middle-gray toned paper or cloth to lessen the depth of the shadows.) Light from a northern window or a lamp should create the best effect for the draftsman: clarity of form, outline, and a sense of drama are to be sought after. While working on the plates in part I you will find examples of various ways to manage lights.

To repeat, all these arrangements must remain absolutely stable throughout the drawing process. Slight changes in the position of the light or the cast can make it impossible to continue a drawing already in progress. Trace the outline of the base of the cast on the bottom of the shadow box just in case the cast gets moved.

Using sticks fastened to the sides of the box, hang a plumb line in front of the cast. Position it so that it cuts through the cast somewhere in the middle and crosses through some important reference or angle points. This real plumb line will be the same as the plumb line (vertical reference line) around which your drawing will be organized. It may take some time to set the cast up in the shadow box.

In drawing from a cast, that is, making a life-size transcription of the cast, the drawing paper on its easel will be placed alongside and just slightly ahead of the subject in the shadow box. If the subject is a cast or a still life, it should be in a setup, either on a stand or in a shadow box. When drawing a live model, the model should be positioned behind the easel, at some distance from which both could easily be seen, so that the apparent height of the model would fit upon the sheet of the drawing paper.

Drawing After a Cast: Positioning the Drawing

After the cast has been set up in the shadow box, the light adjusted, and the easel placed with the drawing board and paper on it set properly next to the shadow box, the drawing process can start. The placement of the paper at the edge of the drawing board (on the model's side) and the drawing board at the easel edge (close to the view of the model) will make it easier to make measurements from the subject and to make visual comparisons of your work and the cast (fig. 45).

Step 1: Draw two horizontals across the paper that define the height of the cast. Since you need a plumb line while drawing the figure, the string of the plumb line is the handiest tool for this step.[53] Use your thumbnails to mark the visible distance on the taut string.

Stretch the string between two hands horizontally across the peak of the head of the model and over the drawing paper. Memorize the path of the line of the string across the paper; step forward and mark the path—one or two marks will suffice.

Step back and use the string of your plumb line to check the mark for accuracy; then lower the string and repeat the process for the lowest point of the feet; do not lower your head for this measurement, just your eyes.

Stand back again and check the marks by holding up the string across the drawing and the cast again. Draw a horizontal through each of the marks, top and bottom.

Step 2: Decide on the placement of the cast's image upon the paper by estimating its width using the taught string or your eye.

Measure the width of the cast at its widest point from your set standing position. Move the extended string over to the paper; decide where it fits most comfortably, but not too far from the edge of the paper nearest the cast. Mark both ends on the paper. Check your measurements.

Step 3: Draw a plumb line (a vertical reference line) from the top line to the bottom line. It should be drawn well enough inside the width limits you have previously set up.

Use the string of the plumb line again to check the width of the figure and its placement on the paper before you draw the plumb line on the paper. You must first pick out the plumb line you want on the subject, a line, say, following the center of balance, preferably one that passes through many or several

useful points on the cast. This can be found and preserved by dropping another plumb line in front of the cast from a stick fastened to the shadow box. Judge where to hang the line from your foot position.

Return to the location of the broadest width that you used earlier when deciding where to place your drawing on the paper. Find by measurement where the actual plumb line on the cast is within that measured width and find the same spot on your drawing by measuring again with your string. Draw the perpendicular through that spot, making sure that it is square with the top and bottom horizontal lines.

As you continue, you must always look at the figure or subject from the same vantage point and with the same stance—feet in position, legs and arms locked and steady, as you hold out the measuring string or needle. With your head always in the same position, look with one eye—always the same eye. You want the middle of the drawing to be straight in front of you. When you look down at the model's feet, for instance, don't drop your head, just your eye. These small practices will soon become habitual and will save you much aggravation.

Fig. 45.
Sight-Size Technique.
Left: measuring apparent distances.
Right: finding an appropriate plumb line (vertical reference line); or checking for vertical elements and angle alignments. Both figures are meant to be working from the same marked foot position on the floor.
Drawing: Graydon Parrish

Drawing After a Cast: Measuring Apparent Distances

Before beginning, measure the model from the plumb line to the widest and lowest points. (1) Look for an important angle, concave or convex, on the contour of the model. (2) From your marked floor position, hold up your plumb line string and make sure that you are holding it horizontally by comparing it with the top and bottom horizontals on the drawing paper. (3) Pick an important point that will help define the shape of the image. Start with the extremities and extended limbs. Move the string—still held horizontally—over the point you wish to record. (4) Make a mark on the plumb line where the horizontal string passes through it and the angle on the cast. Take the length of string (held tightly between the two fingers of your extended hands) and measure the distance from the angle on the cast between your thumbnails and the plumb line hanging before the cast. (5) Keeping your arms extended and the string taut, move the string over the drawing paper; one end of the string should be over the mark on the drawn plumb line, while the other will be over the paper where the contour mark should be. Memorize that spot. Step forward and mark it lightly. Step back and check the accuracy of its placement with the extended plumb line.

Work this way around the figure until you have the shape circumscribed by dots; when you are certain they are all correctly measured and placed, you may connect the dots with straight lines. You can make lines through the plumb line for the slant of the shoulders, hips, or other features. Adding another horizontal or perpendicular vertical may help you deal with some difficult areas. The measuring, placing, and correcting of dots is cumbersome at first, but as you learn the method you will be able to pick out fewer and better points on the contours to work from and to estimate distances more quickly—sometimes with your eye alone. Since there is a lot of stepping back to measure and forward to mark or erase a spot, you should have in your hand at all times the pencil or charcoal, the plumb line, and the eraser so that you can switch instruments without losing your concentration.

Be sure to make these first connection lines straight. The curves can be worked out later. The greater the amplitude of the curve, the more straight lines—connected by points—you will need to outline the curve. One fundamental of Bargue's method is the simplification of complex curves into straights; if one starts drawing a curve, one tends to draw an arc, and it is hard to know where to stop. (As your eye gets experienced, you will be able to connect some of the dots by curves.)

Once a full contour is drawn, it should be carefully checked—through measurement and study all the way around—before features on the inside of the form are put in. Studying your drawing or comparing it with the model in a mirror will help you uncover errors. (A mirror should always be kept handy for checking your drawing.) Refine the outline several times before filling in the curves, putting lines in for the major shadow; then revise the outline again. Once you fill in the major shadow shape, you will see that the contour needs further adjustment.

Keep your dimensions accurate and tight: if the figure spreads just a bit, you will have difficulty fitting the features into the outline and you may even lose the sense of an organic whole. Where it is hard to measure visually, you can resort to a tool for measurements again. Remember that a slightly wider, inaccurate neck may change a young boy into a mature man.

Drawing After Flat Models: Bargue's Plates

The Bargue plates in parts I and III were drawn from the fixed point of view of a stable model; they might have been drawn with sight-size technique or a version of it. One of the main benefits of working in sight-size—besides the production of an accurate image—is the training it gives the eye in measuring visual dimensions. Both to prepare yourself to work from casts and models in sight-size and to benefit from this training of the eye, it is wise to adapt as much of the sight-size technique as possible to the copying of the plates.

Place the plate and the drawing paper side by side on a drawing board, an upright easel, or preferably on a well-lit wall. Locate a good plumb line on the drawing. (You can tape a piece of string in position over the image for the plumb line and for the top and bottom horizontals.) Transfer them to the drawing. Set up comfortable foot positions centered on a line perpendicular to the juncture of the plate and the paper. Using the foot positions will get you used to judging measurements from a distance with a plumb line, memorizing them, stepping forward to record them, and stepping back to correct them. Try to do as much of your work as possible in this manner. At times copying details close up will be necessary, but always step back to judge your work. Stepping back also keeps you conscious of the effect of the whole, which you can further ascertain using a mirror. Check your shadow masses in a black mirror.

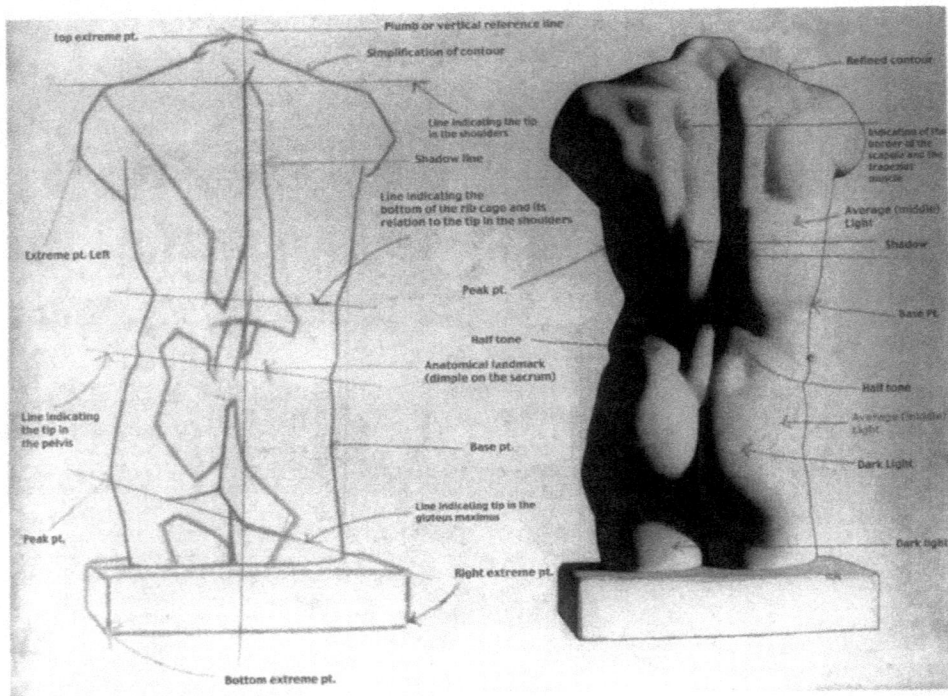

Figure annotations (left drawing):
- top extreme pt.
- Plumb or vertical reference line
- Simplification of contour
- Line indicating the tip in the shoulders
- Shadow line
- Line indicating the bottom of the rib cage and its relation to the tip in the shoulders
- Extreme pt. Left
- Peak pt.
- Half tone
- Anatomical landmark (dimple on the sacrum)
- Line indicating the tip in the pelvis
- Base pt.
- Line indicating tip in the gluteus maximus
- Peak pt.
- Right extreme pt.
- Bottom extreme pt.

Figure annotations (right photograph):
- Refined contour
- Invocation of the border of the scapula and the trapezius muscle
- Average (middle) Light
- Shadow
- Base Pt.
- Half tone
- Average (middle) Light
- Dark Light
- Dark light

Pros and Cons Concerning the Sight-Size Technique: A Dialogue

Using sight-size as the only way of drawing might make practitioners model-bound and interfere with their depiction of objects from memory. Since models are incapable of holding dynamic poses for more than a few minutes, it may delay learning the elements that give motion to a drawing. In addition to increasing the student's dependence upon the model, it also creates a dependence upon ideal conditions—typically those encountered in a studio—such as a controlled light source, an uncluttered and neutral background, and a model trained to hold long poses on a raised platform. However, it does not hinder the depiction of subjects larger or smaller than life size because there are several easy mechanical means of enlarging or diminishing drawn images.

Fig. 46. *Terminology and Concerns in Working from a Cast or Live Model.* The example is taken from the Polykleitan male torso, back view (see plate I, 56). *Annotations:* Graydon Parrish

Peter Bougie, the artist responsible for the fine definition of the sight-size technique at the beginning of this appendix, discussed the merits and disadvantages of the practice with me in an exchange of letters in 2001, from which several excerpts follow. In response to my comment about the innumerable times one wanted to draw something when a sight-size setup (particularly an upright easel) was not feasible, he replied:

"On the slant of the easel, I'll only put in this two cents' worth: a vertical easel is necessary for two reasons. One is so you can step back and look at the subject and draw (with both the subject and drawing in view) side by side without moving your head up and down or left and right. Two, since you're working from a fixed vantage point and measuring, your drawing becomes distorted the more your easel tips away from the vertical, because the top of the drawing is closer to the subject than the bottom.

"Sight-size is very useful in many ways but has definite limitations. It's a good teaching tool and we insist that everyone use it because it sharpens the beginner's eye for proportion relatively quickly and provides an objective context in which to work. It's good for use in the studio in a controlled setting, but it's impractical for landscape painting (not theoretically, but in practical terms) or making studies from life on the fly.[34] I've also noticed that for some students who are naïve (in their drawing experience), or of a strong logical mindset, sight-size gets in the way of seeing when they reach a certain point in their development. They will use the plumb line too much and their eye not enough. I've always thought that sight-size gets you close to where you want to go, in terms of seeing nature correctly, but if you don't step back and compare what you've done to what you see, it can trip you up. In an académie study, if you have a head that's 1/32 or 2/32 too big and a width across the shoulders that is about that much too narrow, the head will look quite large, and you can stand there with your plumb line for an hour and be unable to measure those small fractions with any confidence. You'll just think the head looks big and you won't know why unless you interrelate the parts. So you have to look and compare; that's what it comes down to. And any artist worth his salt ought to regularly practice sitting down with a pad on his lap, or some flat surface, to develop a capacity for gathering information that way, if for no other reason than that situations often call for it.

"I hope I haven't been too didactic. Finally, it's whatever works. But, in my opinion, that 'whatever' has to be grounded in some solid method, or it sounds a lot like the kind of vague instruction people pay for in so many of the art programs out there these days."

"You cut the Gordian knot for me," I replied. "The knot was in my head." Then I continued:

"Sight-size is great for teaching observation and precision. It is also wonderful in teaching because the correction can be precise. I find a problem in sight-size: if carried on too long, the students become model-bound and limited to the poses they can set before them. This keeps them from attempting motion, some expressions, interactions between personages, etc. They just draw and paint models sitting, lying, or standing around. (Gérôme complained that he often couldn't get the good charcoal renderers out of the life class and into painting.) But, still, if you want to be an exacting realist, sight-size shows you the way.

"The Florence Academy of Art (under Daniel Graves) has evening free drawing sessions where the students draw after models with their drawing boards on their laps, a slanted or a straight easel, whatever. These freewheeling sessions occur two or three nights a week, with poses of fifteen minutes to an hour. You stand or sit where you can. I did not realize that this exercise was a natural corrective to the habits of the sight-size technique that were picked up in the daytime sessions at the school.

"The Bargue course, with its mixture of casts and académies, is set up like the private ateliers of the French academy. In Paris the students drew alternately from casts of antiquities and from models, three weeks for each in turn. In Florence students draw from the cast for half a day and from models for the other half. Consequently one could personally move toward realism or idealism in one's personal style. Usually one stopped somewhere in between. Being a purist in either direction could put your style in a straightjacket. Bargue gives you both casts of perfect bodies and parts in the first section and a variety of body types—including the nonideal, aged body—in the third part.

"I am not against other methods nor a partisan of any (although I do naturally prefer and understand best what I was taught, but must protect myself from being dogmatic about it); I think that different methods of drawing from life should just be called methods, none the 'one way,' and that the principles should be recognized as part of the method that organizes work and observation, not as absolutes. The payoff will always be the results.

To which Mr. Bougie replied: "You're right about the shortcomings of sight-size—it's strictly for working in controlled situations, and it does breed a dependence on the model. I'm going to try having students do more work from flat copy of expressive figures, figures in motion, and so on, to try to bridge the gap between the study of nature and its application to making pictures. In doing that, I'm going to compare the two and try to show people how they differ. The trick will be to keep them on track with both the observation and the learning about convention without having the limitations of each method pollute the other, that is, become shortcuts, excuses, or mannerisms in the hands of the inexperienced."

www.ingramcontent.com/pod-product-compliance
Lightning Source LLC
Chambersburg PA
CBHW030821270326
41928CB00007B/832